GENERATION TO GENERATION

CW00742007

Other titles in the Cassell Education series:

P. Ainley: *Young People Leaving Home*

P. Ainley and M. Corney: *Training for the Future: The Rise and Fall of the Manpower Services Commission*

G. Antonouris and J. Wilson: *Equal Opportunities in Schools: New Dimensions in Topic Work*

M. Barber: *Education in the Capital*

L. Bash and D. Coulby: *The Education Reform Act: Competition and Control*

D. E. Bland: *Managing Higher Education*

M. Booth, J. Furlong and M. Wilkin: *Partnership in Initial Teacher Training*

M. Bottery: *The Morality of the School: The Theory and Practice of Values in Education*

G. Claxton: *Being a Teacher: A Positive Approach to Change and Stress*

G. Claxton: *Teaching to Learn: A Direction for Education*

D. Coffey: *Schools and Work: Developments in Vocational Education*

D. Coulby and L. Bash: *Contradiction and Conflict: The 1988 Education Act in Action*

D. Coulby and S. Ward (eds): *The Primary Core National Curriculum*

L. B. Curzon: *Teaching in Further Education* (4th edition)

P. Daunt: *Meeting Disability: A European Response*

J. Freeman: *Gifted Children Growing Up*

J. Lynch: *Education for Citizenship in a Multicultural Society*

J. Nias, G. Southworth and R. Yeomans: *Staff Relationships in the Primary School*

R. Ritchie (ed.): *Profiling in Primary Schools: A Handbook for Teachers*

A. Rogers: *Adults Learning for Development*

B. Spiecker and R. Straughan (eds): *Freedom and Indoctrination in Education: International Perspectives*

R. Straughan: *Beliefs, Behaviour and Education*

M. Styles, E. Bearne and V. Watson (eds): *After Alice: Exploring Children's Literature*

S. Tann: *Developing Language in the Primary Classroom*

H. Thomas: *Education Costs and Performance*

H. Thomas with G. Kirkpatrick and E. Nicholson: *Financial Delegation and the Local Management of Schools*

D. Thyer and J. Maggs: *Teaching Mathematics to Young Children* (3rd edition)

M. Watts: *The Science of Problem-Solving*

M. Watts (ed.): *Science in the National Curriculum*

J. Wilson: *A New Introduction to Moral Education*

S. Wolfendale *et al.* (eds): *The Profession and Practice of Educational Psychology: Future Directions*

Generation to Generation

Maureen O'Connor

Drawing on material and interviews assembled by
Tricia Adams for the LinkAge Trust

CASSELL

Cassell Educational Limited
Villiers House
41/47 Strand
London WC2N 5JE

387 Park Avenue South
New York
NY 10016-8810

British Library Cataloguing-in-Publication Data
A catalogue record for this book is available from the British Library.

Library of Congress Cataloging-in-Publication Data
Available from the Library of Congress.

ISBN 0-304-32682-8 (hardback)
      0-304-32588-0 (paperback)

Typeset by Colset Private Limited, Singapore
Printed and bound in Great Britain by
Biddles Ltd, Guildford and King's Lynn

Contents

Foreword

To be deprived of a grandparent can be almost as grievous for a child as to be deprived of a parent. Grandparents can complement what parents do by just being there when parents are away or absent; by having an easy, warm relationship with children without the primary responsibility for discipline and upbringing; and above all, by having time to be with them. Likewise, to be deprived of grandchildren can be as grievous for a person of grandparent age as it is the other way round for children. The young can keep the old young, or at least give them another sweet taste of what it was once like to be young. The long and the short of it is that there is mutual advantage in a relationship between the generations.

One of the sadnesses of modern society is, therefore, that so many children are without grandparents on the spot and so many people without grandchildren. Hence the move to bring together young people and old in joint activities – this being the function of LinkAge, the charitable trust which has sponsored this book by a well-known writer on education, Maureen O'Connor.

If, when you have read it, you would like to join in yourself and start up a scheme for bringing older people into the lives of younger in schools or the like, or younger people into the lives of older in hospital or homes, you can become a LinkAge Associate by writing to the address below. Once you are an Associate you will get guidance on how to set about the task and be kept in touch with what others are doing.

Lord Young of Dartington (Founder, LinkAge)

Write to: Director, LinkAge, 237 Pentonville Road, London N1 9NJ

Preface

The idea of the young and the old having a valuable and mutually rewarding relationship is not new. Innovation comes from creating ways to sustain that relationship when it is being challenged by changes in society and the family structure. The aim of LinkAge is to respond to the challenge and to find out how to bring the generations together in ways that are appropriate to the present day.

The model of the extended family wherein grandparents and elders play a crucial role to support young parents in the upbringing of children, both with their physical care and the passing on of skills, family history and cultural traditions, would be recognized in most societies around the world. The founder of LinkAge, Lord Young of Dartington, and his colleague Peter Willmott wrote of the importance of this network of support in their 1950s study *Family and Kinship in East London*, and it quite possibly could have been translated into the experience of many other cultures. However, the world is rapidly changing and the repercussions are being felt by the two most vulnerable age groups, the young and the old, separately and also in their relationship with each other. This is not necessarily a bad thing but it does mean the need to adapt.

The extended family still exists, in fact in Britain there are more grandparents around than ever before, but the level and nature of the contact between family generations is altering. Families can become fragmented for a number of reasons, most commonly marital breakdown or a move to seek work and improved living conditions. Divorce and remarriage can bring children an abundance of grandparents, but it can also mean estrangement from grandparents when there is bad feeling between the parents. This is a situation that causes great anguish and heartbreak but so often goes unrecognized. Geographical mobility can be a double-edged sword when one sort of security means the loss of support from family separated by miles or even countries. Get-togethers may be confined to special occasions, and children of immigrant families may never have the opportunity to visit their country of origin or to meet their grandparents.

Other factors seem to conspire to keep the young and old from meeting informally and forming friendships in their daily lives. Community services have become increasingly geared to specific age groups and have led to a form of segregation. The outcome of lack of real contact between the generations is already becoming apparent with misconceptions and stereotyping coming from both age groups. The young are perceived as noisy, undisciplined and potential attackers, the old as useless, cantankerous and hostile. These attitudes do not bode well for the future and obviously something must be done to prepare the children in our schools today for their lives as adults, when they will take responsibility for the financial and physical care of the elderly. This issue is of major importance to Britain and to the rest of Europe, which has a rapidly ageing population. By the year 2005 nearly one in four of the UK population will be over state retirement age. Understanding between the generations is vital, and LinkAge is meeting the challenge of tomorrow by starting that process today.

The United States has recognized the need of more intergenerational contact for many years and has established several interesting schemes that harness the potential of an active older generation to support the young. Examples include a 'Foster Grandparent' scheme which trains and pays a stipend to older volunteers who work with children with special needs. They provide two hours of daily sustained, individual attention to each of two children in school or in hospital. Their role is to be a grandparent in every sense – a caring, stable presence in a child's life.

Some 'Foster Grandparents' enjoy widening their skills, for instance learning to sign in order to communicate better with hearing-impaired children. Some children receive visits in their own homes and in some cases the volunteers work with the family in addressing the problems of abuse and neglect. LinkAge has recently undertaken a feasibility study to see whether a similar scheme would be workable in Britain.

The Columbia University Retired Faculty Community Link-Age Initiative was founded after a survey of retired professors who had remained in the neighbourhood found that a majority were eager to donate their time, energy and expertise by participating in a community activity. Initially the professors lectured or led seminars at schools in the surrounding neighbourhoods; then in 1985 they tackled a serious drop-out problem in the Bronx school district and two mini-schools were established for students who were not reaching their full potential.

The problem of day care has also been addressed with a pilot centre that offers carers provision for their children and elderly relatives under one roof. For part of the day, activities are integrated so that the young and old can be together.

As this book will show, Britain has already begun to formulate some ideas of its own, as have other European countries. This year, 1993, has been designated European Year of the Elderly and Solidarity between the Generations, when there will be an opportunity to share and develop such ideas.

Everyone who was interviewed for the book was very positive about the projects they had been involved in. Anxieties that perhaps the young and old would not get on were very quickly allayed. Though LinkAge is based on the premiss that young and old have much to offer one another, we are constantly surprised at how well children cope with situations that would daunt some adults. To enter a geriatric ward and make contact with people who at first seem unlikely to respond is a challenge in itself and one they meet with refreshing directness. Apart from the affection they show towards their older partners they also demonstrate a good deal of ingenuity in overcoming problems or coming up with new ideas. Teachers usually consider this to be just one of the positive outcomes of taking a classroom activity into this very different setting.

There is currently an interest in the concept of teaching associates – that is, people with a particular skill or profession who can be brought into schools to enhance the curriculum and also bring staff and pupils into contact with other adults and professions. Perhaps this will become the norm and will include older retired people. LinkAge has already demonstrated how well this can work. It would be a terrible waste of human resources if the lifetime skills and experiences of older people were not used to the full, especially in these times when some people take early retirement, and with improved health and longer lives we can expect many years of productive life long after paid employment. There are benefits for the older volunteers too, in feeling valued and having something to pass on to the next generation. If they don't have much contact with their own grandchildren it can give them an opportunity to mix and keep in touch with the younger age group.

Older people also have an asset that younger adults may not possess – time to spare. This is extremely valuable to children, who in a very busy world may have difficulty finding someone who has the time just to sit and listen. This is something that some teachers have requested from LinkAge, specifically for small groups of children with communication problems; as one teacher said, 'The volunteer doesn't need to have any skills, except for the ability to listen and play.' Her particular concern was those pupils who had very little opportunity for conversation or fun at home.

What this book shows, and the work of LinkAge aims to demonstrate, are the opportunities that are there to bring the generations together in new ways that have immense value to both generations and to the professionals who work with them. Much is educational in broad terms and leads to specific academic pursuits. Some schools have engaged in a project solely for the social interaction of their pupils with an older generation. Other schools have involved the whole school in a thematic cross-curricular programme for several weeks. The information in this book about particular schools and places describes the situation at the time it was written. But schools change fast and some of the projects may have come to a natural end. What matters is that they still have value as examples of good practice.

There is some anecdotal evidence that the demands of the National Curriculum have meant that schools are now finding it more difficult to justify or to put into practice projects involving intergenerational links. However, we are assured by Dr Tim Lomas, an Education inspector in Lincolnshire and a member of the National Curriculum History Working Group, and Roy Wilsher, adviser in social subjects, Lothian Region Education Department, Scotland, that there is still plenty of scope within the National Curriculum and the Scottish Education Guidelines for this type of initiative to continue. Their contributions (in Chapter 1) will assuredly aid teachers reading this handbook to bring an intergenerational perspective into their classrooms.

Tricia Adams
Director, LinkAge

Acknowledgements

As well as the many people who provided generous help and information in the research for this book and who are mentioned in the text, particular thanks are due to Hilary Kirkland, Lothian Regional Council; Pam Schweitzer, Age Exchange; Jocelyn Goddard, LinkAge, Oxfordshire; Margaret Macdonald for access to her research; Catherine Mullan, Help the Aged; RSVP; Susan Langford, Magic Me; and the trustees of LinkAge.

Introduction

Being old is:
happy sometimes,
having fun,
it can be like home,
being lively,
being a granny,
having grandchildren,
looking back,
growing grey hair,
playing games,
listen to music,
doing more things,
not being able to jump,
doing dancing,
being a detectif,
keeping fit,
wearing glasses,
boring sometimes,
doing exercises.

(Karen, Gracemount Primary School, Lothian)

In the last hundred years enormous changes in the patterns of family life have been brought about by the education and employment of women, improved health services, divorce, and contraception. Modern women are likely to become grandmothers for the first time after they have returned to work and taken up their own interests, so they have little opportunity to be involved in caring for their grandchildren, especially if the new family has moved away or broken up.

There is much concern about the effect on children of losing contact with their parents, particularly with their fathers, but there is less worry about the distress of grandparents who may lose complete touch with the younger generation.

In spite of Britain's increasing affluence, there are today many lonely old people in hospitals and day centres. At the same time there are many young people at school and in the community who would welcome a chance to make links of friendship between themselves and the older generation. To bring these different needs together a growing number of projects, such as LinkAge, have been developed.

The social changes which have brought us to our present position are complex. Patterns of family life have, for instance, changed markedly as a result of affluence, birth control, and the more independent status of women. Women now often face a long gap between the birth of their last child – likely to have been conceived before they were 30 – and the birth of their first grandchild. The overlap of generations which was common in Victorian times, when women's child-bearing life generally continued at least until the age of 40, has ended, while the wider extended family has become more fragmented.

An increasing proportion of marriages where there are children of school age or younger break up. Much is written about the risk this poses of children losing contact with their natural parents, particularly their fathers. Much less is said about the pain of grandparents and great-grandparents, who may lose touch completely during the traumas of family breakdown, divorce, and the remarriage and changes of home which often follow. By the time we reach old age, it is likely that it will be our great-grandchildren who are still at the nursery or school stage and that the family, now in its fourth generation, will be widely scattered geographically.

For men, the effective age of retirement has dropped dramatically over the past forty years. In 1951, 90 per cent of men between the ages of 60 and 65 were still at work. Only half are today. In 1951, a third of men above retirement age were still working. Only a tenth are now. Simultaneously, life expectancy has continued to rise for men and women, leaving many pensioners facing fifteen or twenty years of retirement.

Of course, for many people a release from any job and from manual labour in particular is a relief. For others the loss of paid work is keenly felt, and not only financially. In the United States a recent survey discovered that there were two million retired people in the population who would like to get back to work, even if only part time. Given a smaller population, perhaps a third of that number could be in the same position in Britain. And with the number of school-leavers available for work still declining, many of the 'young' retired will undoubtedly find work in the 1990s.

Others will not. Some will prefer to find voluntary rather than paid occupations, perhaps because they are financially secure on their pensions or because they wish to 'pay something back' to the community at the end of successful working lives, or for both reasons. Others are already, or will eventually become, too old to undertake anything in the way of a formal occupation, paid or unpaid, but would enjoy and benefit enormously simply from contact with younger people.

Unfortunately, many young people are cut off from older people in their own families and in the community as the retired move into 'sheltered' housing, in the private and public sectors, which may be physically isolated from the rest of the community, and as a minority – about 5 per cent – eventually move into old people's homes and hospitals. This distancing may breed not only contempt but also fear between the generations as some of the case studies in this book will illustrate: fear on the part of the young at the prospect of growing old, ugly and infirm; fear on the part of the old about crime, rowdiness and vandalism, which they tend to blame entirely on the young.

An incident in Scotland early in 1989 pin-points the nature of the problem and also suggests a solution. Older people in the small town of Bonnyrigg in Midlothian had become quite plainly terrified by the behaviour of a group of young people calling themselves the Bonnyrigg Soccer Youths, who had taken to congregating noisily in the town centre every evening to drink, and on occasion vandalize, until the early hours of the morning. An 87-year-old widow complained to the local paper that the boys were 'intimidating' and that she and other residents were afraid to go out at night because of the behaviour of the 'hooligans'. The police were regularly called but had found it impossible to stamp out the problem.

The situation might have continued indefinitely had it not ended in tragedy. The general mayhem involving the Bonnyrigg youths and rivals from nearby Dalkeith ended in the killing of one local boy by another with a kitchen knife. The local community was so shocked by this incident that it collectively took responsibility for solving the problem caused by disaffected young people with nothing to do in the evenings but roam the streets and cause trouble.

Churches and community groups came together to help and the community education provision in the area was extended to try to accommodate the needs of some of the 'gang' which had been involved in the trouble. Even more significantly for the older residents, a special meeting was held to bring together youths and pensioners to discuss their mutual suspicions openly. The older residents discovered that in the flesh the youngsters were not nearly as intimidating as they had believed, and the youngsters were surprised to find support for their desire for better youth facilities in the town. A couple of games of snooker and a chat, it seemed, went a long way to breaking down what had appeared to be an impenetrable wall of suspicion between the generations.

Social change can be seen as both a cause of problems and an opening to new opportunities, as Michael Young (Lord Young of Dartington, a founder of LinkAge) constantly emphasizes. In an increasing number of areas up and down the country this is the opportunity which is being seized by groups who have recognized that if you look at the needs of the older and younger generations together you can, with some energy and lateral thinking, solve a whole range of problems at once.

Intergenerational projects are not new, either in this country or abroad and they follow three broad patterns: schemes which aim simply to foster good social relationships between older and younger people; schemes which involve older people as volunteers working with the young in schools or youth groups; and schemes which bring older and younger people together to explore what the old can remember of their own youth. Of course these objectives are not mutually exclusive and many projects pursue more than one or even all of them. Nor are they all of recent origin. Some go back more than twenty years.

In the United States, a Federal 'foster-grandparenting' scheme which began in 1965 was assigning more than 65,000 children in difficulties to volunteers over the age of 60 by the mid-1980s. Evaluation showed that both the children and their adopted grandparents were benefiting greatly from the scheme.

In Britain, small-scale efforts to start a foster-grandparent scheme were only moderately successful in the late 1980s. LinkAge concluded that intergenerational links were likely to be more successfully made between existing institutions such as old people's clubs, homes or hospitals, and schools and youth groups. This was the basis upon which LinkAge launched two pilot projects in East London and Oxfordshire in 1989.

Elsewhere education authorities and individual schools were moving in the same direction. Help the Aged's Side by Side scheme promoted a wide range of intergenerational experiments in the early 1980s before ceasing operations. In Scotland, the Community Education Service of Lothian Region, which had been encouraging older people into schools and colleges as students since the late 1970s, launched its Young and Old Together project in 1986 to encourage more creative interaction between the generations.

The value of the older generation as volunteers was also gradually being recognized. Speaking at the launch in 1990 of Age Resource, a scheme to raise public awareness of the value of older people to our society, the then Minister of State for Education, Mrs Angela Rumbold, said that older people could contribute in many ways to the quality of education. Schools were already being helped by retired people who acted as governors and assisted in the classrooms in activities ranging from drama to technology. Community Service Volunteers (CSV) had by this time also launched its Retired and Senior Volunteer Programme (RSVP), which encourages the active retired into voluntary activity in schools as well as in the environment, health and community care.

In parallel to all this activity there was a burgeoning interest in reminiscence and oral history throughout the 1980s. Reminiscence work has one foot in institutions which care for older people and one in the academic oral history movement which has begun to record in books, and on tape and film, the memories of many old people about events and social conditions in the recent past.

In hospitals and homes for older people the aim is therapeutic: assisting older people to recall their own past stimulates them and boosts their self-esteem at a time when their mental faculties may otherwise be likely to fade. In schools it reflects a growing interest in local history and in links with local communities, many of which have changed radically since the time when the present generation of schoolchildren's grandparents and great-grandparents were themselves at school. Interest in oral history has been further accelerated by the crop of anniversaries of events surrounding the Second World War, a theme which is proving a fascinating field for mutual exploration by today's schoolchildren and those who were there at the time.

Almost all the projects described in this book which have attempted to measure how far attitudes towards old people can be changed by intergenerational work have discovered that children's initial attitudes to older people can be extremely negative. They can regard old people as helpless, cantankerous, unfriendly, and dependent, and old age as a state to be feared. The 'before and after' poems written by children at Gracemount Primary School around their visits to older people in residential care illustrate this very clearly.

In America, where intergenerational projects of all kinds are now common in a majority of states, specific efforts have been made to include some study of the ageing process and of the needs of old people in the high school curriculum. In Scotland, where social studies are recommended for all 14- and 15-year-old pupils, space has been found for something similar in the Modern Studies syllabus for the Scottish Certificate of Education Standard Grade. In England and Wales, this is made more problematic by the National Curriculum's exclusion of social studies of any formal kind from its list of compulsory subjects. However, other parts of the National Curriculum do encourage aspects of intergenerational work quite specifically. The guidelines for history teaching mention oral history, and specifically the reminiscences and reflections of older people, as a rich source of information on the recent past for younger children at Key Stage 1 and on the twentieth-century content at Key Stage 4. Similarly, the Curriculum Guidance on Education for Citizenship as a cross-curricular theme emphasizes study of the community, the family and public services, and requires opportunities for community work and involvement.

This book is intended as a guide for schools and teachers who feel they want to follow up some of the extremely successful intergenerational work which has already taken place in Britain. A wide variety of institutions and organizations have been involved. Some projects have flourished and then for one reason or another come to an end. Others have started on a small scale and have grown until they have become an integral part of the everyday life of schools.

As is so often the case, the best practice appears to be that which is adapted to the precise circumstances of those who are taking part in a particular place at a particular time. But in bringing together this collection of case studies it is hoped that individuals whose interest in intergenerational work has been sparked will be able to find examples which can provide a starting-point for work which everyone involved agrees leads to a growth in understanding, mutual respect and friendship. These benefits may be difficult to measure but they are obviously none the less worth while for all that.

Chapter 1

The National Curriculum and Intergenerational Work

OPPORTUNITIES FOR INTERGENERATIONAL ACTIVITIES IN THE NATIONAL CURRICULUM

Tim Lomas

Although the National Curriculum may have taken away some of the freedom and flexibility which schools previously had to carry out a range of extended and unusual activities, many opportunities remain to involve older people in the life and work of a school. There is great scope both within the ten compulsory subjects in the English National Curriculum (nine in primary schools) and within cross-curricular dimensions and themes.

It is important to see the opportunities as ranging beyond National Curriculum History. The examples in this book illustrate clearly that many of the activities range over most of the core and foundation subjects. This may be particularly useful in primary schools which are attempting, where possible, to embrace the National Curriculum through topic approaches.

Whilst any one of the core and foundation subjects can involve intergenerational activities, particular benefits seem to be gained in English, where speaking and listening are a compulsory part of the National Curriculum requirement. Music also provides opportunities, as many older people have knowledge of music from the past. There may also be potential in using those with experience of a modern foreign language, especially in areas with a strong multicultural mix. The emphasis in technology is on designing and making and there are examples of collaborative work and discussion on designs and planning by young and old. There are also exciting possibilities in National Curriculum Geography, which ranges over regional, national, European and global areas and which many older people can contribute to. Religious Education, whilst not a foundation subject with programmes of study and attainment targets, is nevertheless mandatory, and links between the young and older people with different beliefs (and even with the same beliefs and values) can be extremely valuable.

It is National Curriculum History, though, which provides particular scope. Indeed, it is difficult to see how it can be covered properly without using the memories of people in the community. The Final Report of the History Working Group noted how:

> the reminiscences and reflections of people provide one of the richest sources of information for the recent past. If used carefully and selectively, oral history can add colour and depth to historical studies. Memories of family, friends and members of school communities can add a new dimension to pupils' understanding.

The examples in this book show that many schools already build oral work into their curriculum. The National Curriculum merely continues this practice. In fact, it provides opportunities throughout the History curriculum between 5 and 16. Adults talking about their past is a compulsory part of Key Stage 1 (ages 5–7). It is also a requirement that pupils consider stories from different periods and cultures, including myths and legends, stories and eyewitness accounts of historical events, and the everyday life, work, leisure and culture of men, women and children in the past, including changes in the lives of their families and of the British people since the Second World War.

Key Stage 2 (ages 7–11) History offers the best opportunities in the unit on 'Britain since 1930', which seeks to establish connections between the present and Britain's recent past – especially the major events and the lifestyles of different groups of people. People of an older generation are likely to have something to contribute on industrial changes, new forms of transport, the impact of the Second World War, changes in family life, migrations, new technologies, environmental concerns, popular culture and the impact of radio, cinema and television. Key Stage 2 also includes a compulsory local history study which schools have to design themselves. This provides good opportunities for an investigation in depth that can make use of oral reminiscences of people in the community.

Key Stage 3 (ages 11–14) provides less scope since it is predominantly concerned with the period beyond living memory. The one exception to this is the unit on 'The era of the Second World War', which allows pupils to talk to others about their memories and involvement in the period immediately prior to, during, and following the War, including the Home Front. Whilst it is likely that many adults would not have been directly involved, many will have attitudes towards the people and events of the time such as the Holocaust, the atomic bombs, and the redrawing of the world map.

Key Stage 4 (ages 14–16) is no longer compulsory for all pupils but, for those choosing to study History, the scope for intergenerational work is considerable because the emphasis of the National Curriculum in this Key Stage is on the twentieth century. Oral accounts are a mandatory source for pupils to explore. The content yields many possibilities for adults to contribute to – the extension of the parliamentary franchise to women; the changing role of the state, including the development of the Welfare State; economic developments and their impact on work, the environment and everyday life; the ways in which cultural, ethnic and religious differences have affected relationships in Britain; mass communications, popular culture, migration and population changes. A local history dimension is also required.

It is important to reiterate, though, that the opportunities extend far beyond National Curriculum History and the other foundation subjects. All the documentation reminds us that these represent only a basic curriculum. Schools also need to consider cross-curricular elements which can play an important part in providing coherence across the curriculum. Although these cross-curricular elements are not statutorily defined, as with the core and foundation subjects, they should be encompassed in a school's overall curriculum. Early surveys by HMI and others suggest that these areas are not being well covered in the early days of the National Curriculum. Intergenerational work can help achieve effective coverage.

The best guidance on cross-curricular work has come from the National Curriculum Council. It has produced a series of booklets offering guidance and there is general acceptance of their suggestions. They distinguish between *cross-curricular skills* (such as communication, numeracy, problem-solving and information technology), *cross-curricular dimensions* (personal and social education, equal opportunities, special needs and multicultural education) and *cross-curricular themes* (economic and industrial understanding, careers education and guidance, health education, education for citizenship and environmental education). Various suggestions are given as to how these might be dealt with; it is expected that many will be covered through the core and other foundation subjects.

Any one of the cross-curricular themes offers great potential for intergenerational work. *Economic and Industrial Understanding*, for example, could involve older people sharing their experiences of work patterns and the lifestyles associated with their work. There could also be opportunities for them to talk about the ways they managed the household economy and how things have changed over the years. They are likely to have experienced periods of inflation and recession and they can discuss the causes and effects. Some will have belonged to trade unions and their roles and attitudes towards these can be discussed. Consumer issues, prices and wages are also relevant to economic understanding and many will be able to talk about such matters with some clarity. They are likely also to be able to contribute to a discussion on the way the business and industrial structure of the local community has changed, such as retailing, mechanization, changes to the environment, the loss of old skills and trades, and the role of politics in the local economy.

The National Curriculum Council's publication *Careers Education and Guidance* makes clear the many opportunities for intergenerational work. Many older people may have personal experience of discrimination at work or unfair practices such as ethnic, gender, or health discrimination. They may be able to point out the way things have changed at work and the reasons for these changes. One example given in the booklet suggests that pupils in Key Stage 2 collect information about work patterns from people who have retired. Work is not just about work activities, it is also about attitudes, and this could lead to interesting discussion between the generations. There may be scope for exploring controversial issues such as conflicts with the environment, the role of trade unions, and the effects of various industrial laws on industry and businesses. It is also important to remember that work interacts with other aspects of life. The relationship between work and a person's other roles and responsibilities, such as citizen, leisure seeker, consumer, parent and householder, can be examined, including ways this has changed over the years.

Health education seems to offer less room for intergenerational work but an examination of family life in the past would be relevant, as would a study of the changes in medicine and public health. The importance of illness in the past would also repay thought, as would changes in the amount of pollution and its effect on health. The best opportunities, though, would probably lie with older people sharing experiences about changes to personal hygiene and habits such as drinking, smoking, diet and healthy eating.

There is an increasing recognition of the importance of teaching *citizenship* in schools. Many have clamoured for it to be given a mandatory slot. This has so far been resisted; the argument used is that much of it would be covered through the core and foundation subjects, especially History. Whichever way it is dealt with, however, there are good opportunities for intergenerational activities. The National Curriculum Council gives many examples, including the changing idea of 'community', such as relationships between individuals, groups and communities, rights and responsibilities. It is important that pupils be introduced to the pluralistic nature of our society through an examination of its social, cultural, religious and ethnic diversity, the tensions, conflicts, co-operation and interdependence. The different generations are clearly part of this diversity. Another recommendation is that pupils understand the nature of family life and the ways it has changed. Older people can clearly bring a valued perspective to this. It may well give some prominence to the changing roles and responsibilities of women in society.

An understanding of a democratic society is also seen as important for young people. Many adults will have personal opinions and experience regarding political systems and processes, pressure groups, trade unions, the nature of authority and human rights. The National Curriculum Council refers to two other dimensions which provide ample scope for intergenerational discussion. Firstly, the citizen and the law – changing patterns relating to employment and leisure over time, including the changing role of women. Secondly, public services. Older people are likely to have clear memories and viewpoints about the nature of these services and how they have changed.

Environmental education can also link the generations. Many people will have witnessed changes to the local environment, through industrial, housing, or transport developments. They are likely to have views about such environmental changes and these can be shared with pupils who will obviously be *au fait* with little more than the present situation. It could lead to discussion as to whether there has been progress or regression and about the ways in which environmental matters have affected the economy, society, and lifestyles.

OPPORTUNITIES FOR INTERGENERATIONAL ACTIVITIES IN SCOTLAND

Roy Wilsher

Although Scotland does not have a National Curriculum, in the sense in which this term is used in England and Wales, there are Guidelines for the age level 5–14 and examination syllabuses for all abilities beyond the age of 14, the operation of which creates a fairly standard framework throughout Scottish Education.

The 5–14 'Guidelines for Environmental Studies' – still in its consultation stage at the time of writing – offers many opportunities for intergenerational activities in and beyond the classroom. In the description of appropriate methodology it is stressed that

> the World beyond the classroom has many rich contexts for learning and teaching, which should be fully utilised. Fieldwork – work in the local area or further afield – will provide opportunities for obtaining first hand experience . . . It can also provide opportunities to meet and talk with people where they work and live.

Some examples of possible strategies are given – for example, 'carry out a survey of local leisure pursuits, modifying questionnaire in the light of responses'; 'research and enact a short play to express views on a health issue'; 'devising a pageant or dramatic presentation for local old people'.

Within local studies pupils will be encouraged to learn about their own past and the past of their own families and communities. Clearly there are possibilities for reminiscence work to provide evidence, for example, 'annual patterns in their lives', 'why certain festivals and customs are celebrated', and so on. The aim is to encourage pupils 'to develop the idea of change in all that they see and experience'.

The Standard Grade syllabus in History, offered at three different levels to cater for the whole ability range, gives even wider opportunities for reminiscence work. A major innovation is the Historical Investigation, which is undertaken on an individual or small-group basis into some aspect of local or Scottish history chosen by the pupil. First-hand evidence is required and this, of course, in the case of the recent past, could include evidence provided by adults. The use of 'recollections both oral and written' is emphasized in the rationale for the course.

Most teachers encourage pupils to choose an aspect of local history for their Historical Investigation. This will often incorporate field work which draws upon reminiscence work as one source of information. For example, a popular 'broad area' is 'Schools and Schooling', which often involves pupils in interviewing elderly people about their school-days. A written presentation of the Investigation is then made and is assessed by the teacher.

Three options within the Standard Grade syllabus itself also offer opportunities for adults to be invited to speak to classes about their experiences of life. These are Unit 1C, 'Changing Life in Scotland, 1880 – Present Day'; Unit 2B, 'Conflict and Co-operation, 1890–1930'; Unit 2C, 'Conflict and Co-operation, 1930–1960'. For example, visits by Second World War veterans to classes studying 2B and 2C to describe their war experiences, or of housewives to describe the privations on the Home Front, are commonplace in many Scottish schools.

At 16-plus pupils divide, taking one of two pathways – either the academic pathway to the Higher Grade and Certificate of Sixth Year Studies or the general studies pathway to modules examined by the Scottish Vocational and Education Council (SCOTVEC). Higher and CSYS History courses remain largely academic in character with virtually no space for reminiscence work. However, certain of the Scotvec modules – in particular the Local Investigations modules – give ample scope for the use of oral history techniques in collecting information which is then presented in the shape of a brief dissertation to be assessed by the teacher, subject to external moderation.

Chapter 2

Bringing Older People In

The notion of opening up schools to the local community has a long and distinguished history in Britain. Henry Morris established the first village colleges in Cambridgeshire before the Second World War. These were to become the model for community schools all over the country, the result either of a commitment to open access by county and city councils, as in Leicestershire and Coventry, or of the individual initiatives of headteachers.

Specific initiatives to bring the older generation into schools on a regular basis seem to be of more recent origin – although as with most grass-roots developments of this kind it is always possible that someone will recall that it was done somewhere thirty, forty or even fifty years ago.

Jane Fryer of Church Cowley St James First School in Oxford is quite clear that the benefits of the scheme she runs to bring older members of the community into school, both as guests and as volunteers, are two-way. The children gain from relaxed extra attention from adults and from becoming more aware of older people's needs as they get to know them. It is, Jane says, a learning situation for them. Older people say how much they enjoy their visits to the school and the friendships they make there. Typical comments include: 'I thought when I retired I would be doing nothing.' 'The welcome they give you when you go in is just wonderful.'

Harvest Gifts, the report of the LinkAge survey into links

Figure 1 *LinkAge volunteer Eileen Robson, a retired professional cook, brings her skills into the classroom at Romney Avenue Infants School, Bristol. (Photograph courtesy of the* Bristol Evening Post *and LinkAge)*

between schools, community education and older people in Oxfordshire, found that the majority of schools claimed to have some links. However, in many cases these were on special occasions such as the Christmas play or the distribution of harvest gifts. Though these were good starting-points and much enjoyed, the report suggested that schools which had taken the contacts further had found greater rewards. For example, when older people had been actively involved in the production of the school play the experience of working together had given many more opportunities for building friendships and achieving a reciprocal relationship between the generations.

This chapter will concentrate on initiatives which have brought the older generation into schools for a variety of reasons, ranging from regular lunch clubs, or participation in specific classes or courses, to the use of older volunteers to help with reading or other aspects of the curriculum.

A great deal of help has been given to volunteer groups by the Retired and Senior Volunteer Programme (RSVP). Launched by Community Service Volunteers, this is a locally organized programme which aims to harness the talents and energies of anyone over the age of 50 who has the time to spare to undertake volunteer work. Support is given by a small paid core team and regional co-ordinators seconded from industry. RSVP local volunteer organizers, who are retired people, recruit and develop projects in their own area with the volunteers working in groups.

This is not an area of work into which volunteers can walk without careful preparation. Many are intimidated by what they hear about new developments like the National Curriculum and the stress that busy teachers are working under. RSVP organizer David Sage in West Yorkshire stresses that a successful project may need several months of careful preparation and discussion. For instance, approval may have to be sought from school governors as well as the head, and if volunteers are to work closely with children they should be screened according to local authority guidelines for those who work with children and young people.

SHARING SCHOOL FACILITIES WITH OLDER PEOPLE

Dunstan Riverside Primary School, Gateshead

The Parent–Teacher Association pioneered community involvement in this school almost twenty years ago. In 1982 the staff decided to give a specific responsibility for community development to one of their number and contact was made with a group of older people who were desperately looking for somewhere to meet regularly. A school was not really what they were looking for. In fact, some found the prospect of even a primary school rather daunting. However, they accepted the invitation.

Conscious of this ambivalence, the school staff made every effort to make their guests feel comfortable. A room was furnished for adults and a kitchen area made available for their use. By the end of the year a second group had been formed and more than fifty older people a week were visiting the school. At this stage, although relationships between the visitors and the school staff were friendly, involvement did not go beyond invitations to the groups to attend important events like Harvest Festival and Christmas celebrations.

Help the Aged's Side by Side scheme to promote intergenerational work in schools was also launched that year and led the school to consider closer contact between the older groups meeting in the school and the pupils. Group members were initially very nervous of the idea of going into classrooms. They felt that they could not take on the role of teacher and feared that children would not welcome them. They were also convinced that they had very little to offer children. Discussion allayed some of these fears and revealed that the best approach would be through the sharing of practical and craft skills.

A great deal of planning went into the initial classroom experiment. Small groups of children were selected to work with the older volunteers – four children with a pair of volunteers for a craft class. The project group worked alongside the rest of the class. It became apparent that initial shyness on both sides soon wore off, and other children quickly became involved with the visitors. Large numbers of children soon found an enthusiasm for some of the old crafts of the area: mat-making, quilt-making, crocheting, and the baking of traditional treats such as Stotty cakes and hot cross buns. The confidence of the older volunteers soon grew so that they could cope with large groups of children without stress. A teacher recorded at the time:

> The relationships within the groups are friendly and conversation flows easily. There is no doubt that the adult skills are being transferred to the children without stress. A most natural process it seems.

Once launched, the involvement of older people in the day-to-day life of the school has flourished. Three groups now meet there regularly, with about eighty older people in school during the course of a week. Many of the original volunteers still help in classes and others have been encouraged to do so.

Major projects have grown out of the original classroom involvement. In 1985 the school staged an Old Time Music Hall, involving twenty senior citizens, thirty-three children and a group of parents who made costumes and helped backstage. Older people were invaluable as 'experts' who knew the songs and remembered how they were performed, as well as performing themselves.

The following year, the school acted as host to a local entertainer and poet, Little Billy Fane, as part of a Writers in School project. Children studied their local environment, past, present and future, and worked closely with older people discussing and recording their reminiscences of the past and going with them on expeditions to places of interest in the area. This culminated in a stage production written by Billy Fane and performed by the children and older people together. The script, based on the children's own writing, drew heavily on the lives and experiences – and hopes – of older people.

Dunstan Riverside School received the National Curriculum Award for its intergenerational work in 1987.

Beeslack High School, Penicuik

Beeslack was not originally designated a community school by Lothian Regional Council, but as a purpose-built high school in an Edinburgh dormitory suburb it was provided with specific areas for community use: a lounge, swimming-pool and sports hall. The whole school is available for community activities out of school hours. Community activities and school activities come under the joint control of the head, but staff are not on specific 'community school' contracts that would give them time to facilitate community activities.

In spite of these limitations, the school community facilities are well used, particularly by the older generation. Adults are free to join school classes where there is space. The local photographic club has equipped a dark-room at the school for joint use.

The advantages for children, staff say, are threefold: they gain from working in an 'open' building and coming into frequent contact with adults, including the older generation; older children benefit from having adults in class – their influence is calming and in discussion-based subjects their contribution, often based on experience, can be particularly valuable; and for the fourth year (15–16-year-olds who may be desperate to leave school), the idea is easily conveyed that education can continue long after school-days. Young people have become volunteers at the swimming classes for older people on Tuesday afternoons, and at a Disabled Club on Sundays which includes older people from a local residential home.

Members of the Over-50s group, which meets regularly at the school, do not meet pupils in a structured way but appreciate being asked to help with one-off activities and projects and enjoy the social contact which arises naturally in the shared environment. They have been asked for help with reminiscence work by the Beeslack history department and by a local primary school which was built on the site of a coal-mine where there was a major disaster in the last century. They were asked about conditions in the mines and industry when they were young. Members of the Over-50s art group were welcomed into the school's art department to gain new ideas and for some help with pottery.

Older pupils at the school are involved in community service and some work with older people in the local geriatric hospital. School staff say that this can be a very positive experience in breaking down barriers between the generations. One boy developed an ambition to become a nurse as a result of his voluntary work.

At the end of the school year the timetable is suspended and various activities are provided for pupils in which community members (of any age) are invited to participate. Older members of the Over-50s group still speak warmly of their experiences hill-walking and skating with the younger generation. Contacts – even informal ones – are obviously appreciated, as these comments show:

> You get a good relationship between the generations. Some of the children are from families with no grandparents locally, and I think they appreciate us.

> The swimming session means that I can come swimming with my grandchildren.

> I meet some of the boys from the school at my bowls club – they greet me in the corridor like a friend, and we play sometimes across the generations, on equal terms.

The history department at the school has made use of the Over-50s reminiscence work for its study of local history in the first half of this century. Some older people have provided several pages of reminiscences about their childhoods, their first jobs, and outings and holidays in the area. The following is a brief reminiscence by Jessie McKenzie of her Edinburgh childhood in 1924:

> We lived in a 'stair' and we were on the second landing. The neighbours were all 'aunties' and I was more often than not in one of their houses. Everyone in the stair knew all the comings and goings. We held back green [back yard] concerts and charged for them. Quite a lot of laughs were had at some of the performers. The local policeman was both liked and feared. He put your name in the book if you misbehaved. He was also a person you could approach if you had any problems. The same 'bobby' was always around. People were poor but they all helped one another in those days.

Icknield School day centre

A day centre for older people was opened in 1985 at the Icknield School and Centre for Community Education in Watlington, Oxfordshire. Initially this was little more than a luncheon club run by volunteers, with some support from social services. Within two years the number of people attending on each Wednesday had grown to more than forty, and the centre was being run by a paid organizer and three volunteers.

Peter Davies, former head of Icknield, puts the success of the venture down to two major factors: the environment, and curriculum involvement in the school as a whole. The environment, he thinks, was crucial. The centre was set up at the heart of the school in a classroom. Grants from Age Concern and the county council's Community Education Development Fund allowed the school to carpet the room and the surrounding area and redecorate. When the room was not being used by the centre (i.e. every day except Wednesday) it was used as an ordinary classroom. It thus provided a comfortable environment for older people at the heart of a busy school, and also offered an enhanced environment to pupils and staff for a large part of the week. Peter Davies is eloquent in describing the effect of the centre on the school:

> There was thus a common sense of pride which crossed a generation and welded together young and old in their common right to be. The classroom looked out onto a little grassed quadrangle where students gathered in breaks. I would often see the old people craning and gazing with interest. As they went about their business youngsters would wave at neighbours and grandparents. There were proper facilities – a disabled toilet and so on – so that older people felt comfortable. The involvement of the young with older people grew gradually, but the human desire to care and protect was spontaneous and happened because the centre was in the busiest part of the school. Youngsters never ignored older people moving slowly on two sticks or in a wheelchair. Older people were more likely to be faced by a surfeit of assistance than distressed because of neglect.

Involvement with older people within the curriculum also developed slowly, Mr Davies reports. The first developments came in the most obvious areas, with the history department making use of the personal recollections of some of the older visitors to the school, including one man who had managed to fight as a private on both sides during the Second World War. Students also became voluntarily involved with the centre either as part of their formal Personal and Social Education programme, or as voluntary helpers on an extended basis. One boy used to return to school seven miles by bike to attend sessions at the centre during the school holidays.

Gradually other school departments became involved. The music department, followed by dance and drama, realized the advantages of having a 'captive' audience on site, to evident appreciation by the older people. The Special Needs department began to use the centre as a resource through which slow-learning children could gain experience in maths and practical skills and learn through conversation with older people who had time and patience to spend with the youngsters.

Peter Davies believed that the success of the project at Icknield hinged upon the value that older people added to the life of the school and how that added value could be recognized and harnessed. He foresaw potential developments in more community projects, joint reading schemes, imaginative writing – particularly of biography – and social studies.

After Mr Davies left the school the funding of the project was taken over by Age Concern.

Hatfield High School, Doncaster

Hatfield High School had already placed a high priority on community involvement when in 1981 it decided to look for ways to involve older people in particular more closely in the life of the school. A preliminary meeting to which Over-60s groups in the community were invited uncovered a genuine enthusiasm for making the school the focal point for a variety of social and educational activities involving older people. Since then a range of activities, some one-off, some long-term, have evolved, and more than two hundred older people from the neighbourhood have been involved with children of all ages in the school.

A hundred older people, seventy-five third-year pupils (13-year-olds), and six staff were involved in the Local History Project. This aimed to use the wealth of personal knowledge possessed by older people to build up a dossier of information on the local area. An introductory get-together was followed by classroom sessions involving pupils and older people working side by side. Older people were asked to bring items of historical interest into the classroom and ultimately 400 household items were loaned to the school, which in its turn mounted a display at a local museum. The project lasted six months and the school regarded it as highly successful, both in academic terms (having given a unique insight into local life), in terms of the pupils' motivation, and in terms of the personal relationships between young and old which were established by the project.

The school also runs a Sixteen–Sixties Club. This is based in its youth centre, which is purpose-built and integrated into the main school complex. It offers a variety of sports and leisure facilities, comfortable sitting areas, and the opportunity to provide light refreshments. The objective was to offer older people a chance to share these facilities and in particular to attract the isolated, house-bound and lonely older people in the neighbourhood.

The project was launched with four objectives: to introduce older people to the school and encourage them to use the youth centre; to enable young and old to meet socially and develop a better understanding of each other; to provide a venue for lonely older people who had little opportunity to meet with others; and in the long term to use the club as a basis for introducing older people to aspects of the school curriculum in which they might like to participate. There are now ninety regular members and the club has become an established part of school life.

Relationships between the pupils and older people are warm, and the organization and routine tasks such as making refreshments are shared. It has become an important element in the life of some lonely old people for whom it is their only 'afternoon out'. Outings organized by the club take older people on visits that they would almost certainly not consider on their own.

A group of sixty pensioners and their fifth-year escorts spent an afternoon at Doncaster's new leisure centre in the summer of 1990. They toured the swimming area, skating rink, snooker hall, health club and other facilities, and reached some succinct conclusions about its modern design. As one put it: 'Whoever designed this wants his head looking at', while another was more impressed: 'I like it. Very modern and spacious.' At the end of the visit sixteen older ladies were discovered to be missing from the party. They were found trying out the apparatus in the body-building area, aided and abetted by some of the young men who were body-building there. The visit was voted a huge success.

At the beginning of the 1990/91 school year, Hatfield High School was planning to increase its community involvement. Future plans for involving older people in the life of the school included:

1. Opening the school library to older people, both to enable them to borrow books and for use as a reading room. The librarian has created a sitting area and is purchasing daily newspapers for all tastes.
2. Inviting older people to act as volunteer library assistants.
3. Extending the school's invitation to older residents to take lunch at school one day a week. Lunch is taken in the school dining hall with senior pupils.
4. Developing plans for an 'Older Watch' scheme. This would involve pupils 'adopting' an older person who would be visited for a short time on the way home from school, as children might naturally visit a grandparent. The school sees advantages in breaking down the isolation of some housebound older people and in providing additional security for them by means of regular visits.
5. Transforming a large classroom into a 'community lounge' which could be used by local groups, including older people. Older people would be invited to help in the planning, renovation, and management of the new facility.

SHARING SCHOOL MEALS

Lunch clubs in Oxfordshire schools

As part of LinkAge's pilot project in Oxfordshire, the organizer, Jocelyn Goddard, conducted an informal survey of schools to discover how many were inviting older people into school premises for lunch on a regular basis. She came up with a provisional total of eighteen, both primary and secondary, and a wide variation in approaches.

At *Peers School, Littlemore*, lunches are available in school for pensioners once a week and work is being done on a Meals on Trays scheme. At *Bishop Kirk Middle School, Oxford*, now reorganized, senior citizens were invited to come to lunch any day, and four or five generally turned up. They were served by fourth-year (13-year-old) pupils. At *St Michael's School, Steventon*, a dozen visitors come to lunch once a month and half as many once a fortnight (by popular demand). They eat with the children and sherry and coffee are served (to the adults!). At *Wooton Primary School* the cookery club prepares lunch for four older visitors once a week. They are served and entertained by the children after the normal school meal. At *Fitzharry's School, Abingdon*, fourth-year pupils entertain older guests to lunch and provide some shared activity afterwards as part of their pre-vocational course. Shared outings have also been arranged.

This is how *Drayton Primary School* describes its luncheon club in its school prospectus:

> A strong link has been established between the children and the senior citizens of the village by the Luncheon Club, which takes place at school twice a month. Children are involved in the club, greeting the senior citizens on arrival, waiting on them at table and sharing conversation over lunch.
>
> A group of parents organise this part of school life, providing transport, help in the kitchen and dining room and generally ensuring the smooth running of the club. If you are free between 11 a.m. and 1 p.m. on Tuesdays and Fridays, do come along and help.
>
> Sometimes the children organise an entertainment for their guests, which is much appreciated, and, of course, a welcome is extended to them to look around the school or stay and get

involved with the children. A special invitation to all school events is given to the senior citizens (see Figure 2).

The lunches are paid for by the senor citizens themselves, whilst a raffle provides funds for sherry, coffee, etc. At Christmas time extra funding from the community enables us to provide a special Christmas lunch.

The Luncheon Club is the highlight of the month for many senior citizens and children. Close friendships have developed over the years and are valued by young and old alike.

If you know anyone who may like to join us, please let us know.

At other schools, lunch clubs operate without the specific participation of the school meals staff or teachers. At *Banbury School*, which has a community tutor, students prepare lunch once a week for ten members of the British Pensioners Trade Union Action Association. Pensioners arrive at about 11.15 for coffee and biscuits and an informal chat before lunch. At midday they sit down with students for lunch with a menu which has ranged from Italian dishes to traditional English fare. As one pensioner commented to the local newspaper: 'It's the treat of the week!' At *Bartholomew School, Eynsham*, a day centre for older people runs on the school campus once a week. Lunch is prepared by volunteers.

Jocelyn Goddard believes that as older people become more used to the idea of coming into school – not easy for some whose last contact with a school might have been more than half a century ago – they may begin to build up relationships with children and staff and further involvement may follow. Her aim in Oxfordshire is to establish a network of schools involved in lunch clubs for their mutual interest and support. Lunch clubs, she thinks, are a very effective way of bringing the generations together in an informal and uncomplicated manner. As one Oxfordshire school put it: 'The Luncheon Club is the highlight of the week for many senior citizens and children. Close friendships have developed over the years and are valued by young and old alike.'

Jocelyn Goddard categorizes the benefits as threefold:

1. It extends links between schools and their community: many schools already have links with older people through links with a sheltered housing scheme, through volunteers in the

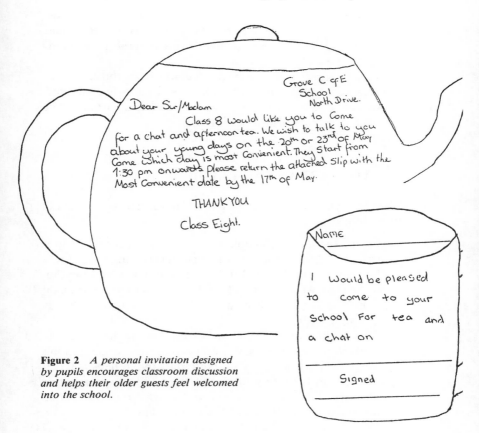

Grove C of E
School
North Drive.

Dear Sir/Madam

Class 8 would like you to come for a chat and afternoon tea. We wish to talk to you about your young days on the 20th or 23rd of May Come which day is most convenient. They start from 1:30 pm onwards Please return the attached slip with the Most convenient date by the 17th of May.

THANK YOU

Class Eight.

Name

I would be pleased to come to your School For tea and a chat on

Signed

Figure 2   *A personal invitation designed by pupils encourages classroom discussion and helps their older guests feel welcomed into the school.*

classroom, or through grandparents who bring children to school and take them home again either occasionally or regularly. The club provides a focus for these links.

2. The greater contact between the generations made possible by a regular lunch club helps to break down misconceptions and misunderstandings between the generations. There is anxiety in some places about 'granny-bashing' or attacks on, and thefts from, older people. Older people may also have misconceptions about modern schools and teaching

methods. Closer contact enables schools to reassure older people and 'set the record straight' in areas of misunderstanding between old and young.

3. Some children may benefit particularly from the chance to talk to an additional adult, even if only for a few minutes. All will be encouraged to see their school as a friendly place which welcomes visitors of all ages.

HOW TO START A LUNCH CLUB

This is Jocelyn Goddard's seven-point plan for setting up a school lunch club:

1. Discuss the idea with cook and kitchen staff if their help is needed. Their co-operation and enthusiasm are vital. More than one school lunch club has been initiated by an enthusiastic cook who is aware of need in the community. It might be helpful for a teacher and cook to visit a school already running a club.

2. Consider how many extra lunches and visitors the school can comfortably accommodate, and how often. Some schools prefer to have a few visitors frequently; others a larger number (up to twenty or thirty) at fortnightly or monthly intervals. If the club is very successful, what is the maximum number which could ever be accommodated?

3. Who is to be invited and how do you get in touch with them? Members of the school can probably come up with a small number of names themselves – grandparents who live locally are an obvious starting-point. Some schools already have lists of older people to whom they distribute gifts at Harvest Festival or Christmas time. Other sources of 'customers', or information about customers, are existing luncheon clubs, which might have waiting lists or be glad of another venue; Age Concern; the social services department; local churches; or the local Over-60s club.

4. These contacts may also be able to offer advice on the most suitable day of the week to offer lunch (i.e. not a day when Meals on Wheels are available).

5. Initial organization may be time-consuming: where will the guests leave their coats? are the chairs big enough? how do you know how many extra lunches will be needed? But most schools report that once the initial work has been done, a club generally operates with the minimum of organization.
6. Except in small villages, transport can be a problem. In Oxfordshire, transport to school lunch clubs is generally provided by some other volunteer group – either parents, or Age Concern, social services or the Red Cross.
7. The School Meals Service may not be able to offer any subsidy for meals for older people. Some schools have got round this by providing a subsidy themselves from school funds or from a regular raffle, and where this is the case they often feel able to offer a glass of sherry and a coffee as a supplement to the school meal.

OLDER PEOPLE AS STUDENTS

Somerset community education schemes

In Somerset, the local authority has been pursuing a policy of opening up its schools to all members of the community since 1974. Projects are not aimed specifically at older people, but a number of schools report that older people are taking advantage of their open-door policies. As the chief education officer, Jennifer Wisker puts it, 'education should be a seamless robe covering everyone from the youngest children to people in old age.'

Many Somerset secondary schools welcome adults into normal classes. Some, like the *Burnham Community Education Centre*, have laid on classes such as Cookery for Men, which have proved particularly attractive to older people. At *Whitstone School, Shepton Mallet*, the community education tutor, Daphne West, has developed an Open Learning scheme which is also particularly useful to people who are not mobile and cannot attend classes in school regularly.

Subjects covered include word-processing, Russian, chemistry and history. Courses are offered at a level suitable for beginners, for those simply learning out of interest, and for those wishing to obtain qualifications. They work on a standard self-study model, with work-packs supported by regular tutorials at a school or college. Enrolment is flexible enough to allow students to start at any time of the year, and students have access to their school or college's library and other resources.

Most students are offered a thirty-minute tutorial every three weeks at times mutually convenient to the student and the tutor. If a student is house-bound tutorials can be arranged at home. Older people particularly appreciate the flexibility of a system which means that they do not have to go out for classes after dark. Obviously an open learning course requires a high degree of commitment from the student but conversely the student can dictate the pace of learning. It can go as quickly or as slowly as the student chooses. So far the youngest student enrolling for an open learning course has been aged 16, the oldest 85.

OLDER PEOPLE AS VOLUNTEERS

St Cuthbert's Primary School, Drumlanrig

Pat Doward, class teacher for P5 (9-year-olds) at St Cuthbert's, agreed to take a retired person into her class for a specified period as part of the Side by Side project in the region. 'I think I thought of it at the start as a sort of "adopt a granny" situation,' she said later. Contact with the Community Education Service resulted in not one but three older ladies arriving in the class a week later bearing the news that another three would also like to come. Only at this stage, Mrs Doward says, did she realize that there would need to be some careful planning if the project was to work. It was eventually agreed that the volunteers would join the class every Thursday afternoon for the summer term.

Activities varied from week to week and included group sessions during which the visitors very successfully taught the children to knit; a session making rosettes for the town festival; an outdoor expedition 'nature spotting', during which the ladies' local knowledge was much appreciated by the children; and a session when the whole class – and volunteers – worked with clay.

Summing up, Mrs Doward concluded in her report that the whole exercise had been extremely worth while, and very much a two-way experience for children and volunteers. The following extract from her report describes the session with clay, which none of the visitors had ever worked or played with before.

Later two ladies made remarks which made me feel that they had really entered into the class situation. 'I can't make very much because she's got a bigger piece of clay than I have!' and 'Will we be allowed to take something home?' Gone was the quiet serenity of the knitting sessions. The ladies chatted and laughed as time went on. One little girl remarked 'They are very noisy, Mrs. Doward, you'll have to split them up.' The afternoon was voted an enjoyable success.

Warrington summer play scheme

In Warrington, a group of older tenants on one of the town's housing estates set up a group which ran a six-week-long series of activities for children and young people over the summer holiday period. Three sessions a day offered activities ranging from story-telling and painting, a teddy bears' picnic for the under-5s, computer sessions, discos, and a series of sports events every evening. Children had to have parental permission to take part and a membership card – which could be withdrawn in the event of 'trouble'. Joint activities continued after the summer with outings and a children's Christmas party.

Glasgow Day Training Centre

In Glasgow, an RSVP group has become involved in work with young people with learning difficulties at a Day Training Centre. Their work on basic literacy and numeracy with the students was recognized locally by the award of a 'Caring Cup' by the *Glasgow Evening Times*.

Bingham Community Education Centre and school

The Bingham CE Centre is built on the same site as the local primary school, serving a council estate which has recently been rebuilt and refurbished. It provides premises for a range of community groups – mothers and toddlers, young unemployed, and older people. A series of youth clubs use the building most evenings.

The lunch club which meets there twice a week brings in a regular group of older residents from the estate who have begun to involve themselves in school activities on a fairly informal basis. They were first invited into a class which was studying pre-war education. This involved a visit to the Edinburgh education museum, where replica classrooms have been set up. Some lunch-club members accompanied children on this visit and later joined them in a classroom discussion of schools then and now. This developed to the point where older women demonstrated old games to the children – bools (marbles), girds (hoops), skipping ropes, and whips and tops.

The relationships made between the generations seem likely to last, as the following two comments testify:

> I've had two visitors, two little girls who seem to have adopted me. There's no Mrs Pratt – it's Chrissie. But I don't mind that at all. That's the modern way.

> We made friends at the school. There was one little boy in the class who knew me and he had to have me in his group. He was very proud of me.

Church Cowley St James First School, Oxford

It is Friday afternoon and there is a 'tea-party' in the school hall. The hosts are 7- and 8-year-olds and the guests older people from the local community, some of them grandparents of children at the school. If a 'granny' is there for tea, a grandchild is allowed to join her during the afternoon whether or not it is the child's turn to act as host. There are tea and cakes available, and the groups round the tables – young and old together – are also engaged in various educational board games. The guests then stay in school for the regular Friday afternoon Family Assembly service at which the children show off their work to parents and friends.

This is a regular event at Church Cowley St James, where older volunteers also help in class with reading and sewing. The school had always invited the local community to its 'big events' such as Harvest Festival and the Christmas play, and it had parents helping in the classroom. When Jane Fryer was given an extra allowance to develop community links further, she regarded the involvement of older people as a natural progression.

> We identified likely local residents through our chairman of governors who is a local man. We sent out invitations and offered transport, because for many older people that is a problem, and we put posters in local shops and the community centre. I then discussed with staff events where senior citizens could be included, and how they could help in class. Most of the people who come are women, many are grannies of children at the school.

The scheme is now run mainly by parent volunteers who make the Friday afternoon tea and help with transport. Jane's job is mainly liaison, she says. Transport is the biggest problem: even with the help of local volunteer transport organizers she still finds it takes her away from her class for a worrying amount of time. It also makes follow-up difficult. One regular visitor to the school is now confined to her home in a wheelchair. The children cannot visit her in school time, although they would like to, because it would need supply teacher cover to allow Jane to take them.

HARNESSING OLDER PEOPLE'S SKILLS

The creative crafts project

This was an experiment launched by Help the Aged as part of its former Side by Side scheme. The objective was to set up situations in which young people in school could learn alongside older people from the local community in a variety of contexts. Some interested schools contacted older people through contacts they already had in day centres, lunch clubs, etc. Others sent out informal invitations like this one:

> If you are a senior citizen who likes talking and working with children, aged 7 to 11, why not join us this term? We have in mind making costumes, both for the Carnival and a play we are producing later this term, but there are other activities going on where help is needed. One lady, for example, is teaching some children to knit. If you would like to come for school dinner, you would be very welcome on Tuesdays or Thursdays during term . . . The children will be delighted to see you, will join you for dinners and gladly give you an escorted tour round the school afterwards.
>
> *Question*: Why not come along and help us make some simple play equipment for the handicapped?
>
> *When*: Mondays, for four weeks: 22nd and 29th June, 6th and 13th July.
>
> *Time*: 1:30 p.m. – 3 p.m.
>
> In which area would you prefer to help? Home economics, metalwork, needlework, woodwork? Please state your preferences in order – that is 1st, 2nd, 3rd and 4th. If you have not done any of the above subjects in school, don't worry! The work is simple and there will be plenty of help available.

The Help the Aged organizers soon discovered that there was no shortage of enthusiasm amongst schools or volunteers for this sort of project. A group of junior children in Cambridge worked with older people on a collage for a nearby special school. A large comprehensive school involved pupils and older volunteers in making wooden clock jigsaws for handicapped children, special domino sets for the blind, and rag dolls, each made to an individual design. The sessions ended with tea and biscuits and a social get-together. Another school offered volunteers a choice of activities: toy-making, crochet, tapestry, weaving, cookery, woodwork and metalwork.

Laura Gamble, Help the Aged's education officer at the time, concluded:

> One of the most encouraging aspects of the reports from all the schools taking part has been the way the confidence of the old people has increased. Some of them were understandably quite diffident at first – many had not been inside a school for twenty or thirty years. But after even a few weeks, they began to see how valuable their skills really could be, especially where the 'tradi-

tional' crafts were concerned – for example: crochet, patchwork and tapestry. Many old people regard these skills as so basic that they take them for granted: they were delighted to find them so much in demand. In much the same way, children take for granted the kind of equipment found in most schools today, but many older people were amazed at the range of choice that modern craft rooms can offer and enjoyed trying their hand at some of the newer ideas.

As with so many intergenerational schemes, in some schools the initial project led on naturally to an extension. One of the schools involved based a needlework course on a nearby sheltered housing development, where residents have joined in enthusiastically in making collage pictures, lavender bags and pin-cushions, calendars and table mats.

Lees First School, Keighley

RSVP volunteers have helped slow readers, prepared equipment for maths work, and undertaken 'domestic chores' around the school. Their work is carefully reviewed and integrated into the normal work of the school. As one teacher said: 'Volunteers can carry out very practical individual work with children that will enable us to teach.'

Other RSVP groups

An early RSVP group in Cambridge ran a highly successful project making dressing-up clothes for a local primary school (see Figure 3). Old sheets and cast-off clothing were turned into nurses' uniforms, capes and cloaks and ballet tutus, which were shared amongst all the children in the school. The 'sewing ladies' were thanked personally by the children and one of the teachers wrote:

> We have two ballerinas constantly prancing around with a well-organised waiting list queuing behind. The outfits are never in the dressing-up box. One of the new mums told me that her daughter was ready for her second day at school at 7.30 a.m. so that she could be sure to get a turn early on!

Figure 3 *An RSVP group in Cambridge helped newcomers to the reception class of a local primary school overcome their nerves by making irresistible dressing-up clothes that had them queuing at the door. (Photograph courtesy of RSVP)*

This enterprise is to continue with RSVP volunteers going back to the school to take groups of older children for embroidery lessons.

In Bristol, a local RSVP group has set up a scheme to provide schools with equipment which was beyond their budgets but which could be made from scrap materials. One school benefited from three new bookcases; another from a child-size 'telephone kiosk', complete with cast-off telephone, made from an old cupboard which the RSVP co-ordinator rescued from a skip.

In Basingstoke, the head of *Fairfield County Primary School* set up a group of a dozen older volunteers by contacting clubs for older people and advertising in the local paper. The group refurbished disused rooms about the school to provide space for photography, cookery and sewing, organized with the help of the volunteers. Design technology, money management and self-expression, first aid, music appreciation and current affairs classes followed. All pupils now participate, and in co-operation with school staff the volunteers have also organized visits to local libraries, civic offices, and the magistrates' court.

LinkAge older volunteers have been welcomed into schools in Oxford, Bristol and the London Borough of Tower Hamlets. This worked most successfully when the needs of the school were matched with the skills and interests of the volunteers so that there were mutual benefits for all concerned.

In Tower Hamlets, where the majority of children live in flats with very little access to green space, a number of schools surveyed asked for older volunteers who would help build and maintain a school nature garden. Ann Ogunnusi, a retired microbiologist, was able to do just that for *Olga Primary School.* She was also living in a flat close to the school and frustrated by not having access to a garden of her own.

Ann's placement became even more successful as the confidence of the teaching staff in her ability to work with the children grew. From outdoor activities growing plants and identifying 'bugs', she moved to practical experiments in the classroom and visits to Spitalfields City Farm (see Figure 4). She is now a valued member of the school.

In Oxford, volunteer Arthur Exell has become an equally valued member of the school community at *St John Fisher RC*

Figure 4   *Retired microbiologist Ann Ogunnusi introduces inner-city children to creatures large and small at Spitalfields Farm and the school nature garden as a LinkAge volunteer at Olga Primary School, East London. (Photograph by Richard Madden; used by courtesy of LinkAge)*

Figure 5 *LinkAge volunteer Arthur Exell has become a valued member of St John Fisher School, Oxford, where he helps pupils improve their communication skills and brings first-hand experience to history projects. (Photograph courtesy of the Oxford Times and LinkAge)*

Primary School. Arthur has worked with a class teacher as a 'primary source' for local history projects, stimulating children's interest in his eighty years of memories, and has helped a small group of children improve their communication skills (see Figure 5).

Both these examples illustrate the trend for older people to become involved in schools in a much more active way, rather than simply as visitors there to be 'entertained'. LinkAge's Oxfordshire survey (*Harvest Gifts*, published in 1991), commissioned by the local education authority, bore out this trend:

> A glance at the list of activities currently being undertaken by retired volunteers in Oxfordshire schools is reassuring. The schools are making use of many skills and interests to be found within this generation, the Third Age. Older people in twos and threes are coming in to help in over one third of the schools questioned.

Chapter 3

Going Out to Older People

Secondary schools now have a long-established tradition of community service, which has very often involved them in visiting older people either in their homes or in sheltered accommodation or old people's homes. The primary objective has usually been to offer 'service' – shopping, gardening or decorating for older people who are house-bound or unable to undertake heavy work at home – and assistance with 'care' chores in an institutional setting. There are some difficulties in this approach if younger people are not carefully prepared to meet older people. There is an obvious risk that older people will feel patronized or worse if young people descend on them to 'do good violently'.

From the range of case studies collected in this chapter it is clear that many schools are now approaching community work schemes with some sensitivity, and also that the aims and objectives of involving young people with the older generation out of school are changing. There is much more emphasis on mutuality: a much stronger sense that young people as well as older people can and will benefit from contact, a much wider range of activities linking the generations and a conviction that the older generation has a great deal to offer the young in the way of shared experience and history.

VISITING OLDER PEOPLE

LinkAge in Tower Hamlets

Tower Hamlets in the East End of London was one of three areas selected for a series of pilot projects by LinkAge to explore ways of improving contact between young and old. One model was to foster links between existing institutions (such as schools, nurseries and youth groups) and pensioners' clubs, residential care homes, hospitals and sheltered housing.

  Bethnal Green Hospital proved to be the most fertile ground for the project. The hospital had a large population of elderly patients, many of whom were in long-stay wards. The hospital's attitude was summed up by the comment of a member of the management team: 'If the patients cannot go out, we encourage the world to come in.' Links were made with a range of age groups in nursery, primary and secondary schools. Subsequently a relationship was formed with a further education college.

University House Nursery

During the summer months five wheelchair-bound patients spent an afternoon each week in the nursery school gardens. The children enjoyed having an audience to wave to as they rode around on tricycles and a good supply of laps to sit on when cuddles were required. For the patients it seemed an emotionally rewarding time and as one woman in her eighties said through happy tears: 'I never thought I'd be holding a baby again in my lifetime.'

St John's Primary School

St John's was just four minutes' walk away from Bethnal Green Hospital and when LinkAge approached the school they found that contacts already existed. The previous Christmas 8- and 9-year-olds had visited the wards to sing carols, and the head-teacher was very keen to set up regular long-term links.

Figure 6 *Pupils from St John's Primary School left their classroom on one afternoon a week to share a wide range of activities with elderly patients during a LinkAge project at Bethnal Green Hospital, East London. (Photograph by Jo Booth; used by courtesy of LinkAge)*

The project was developed by the school with the continuing help of LinkAge. Preparatory work on older people and ageing was done in the classroom for two sessions before the first visit by a class of 9- and 10-year-olds. The children were encouraged to ask questions about the difficulties of old age and how they would cope with them. This developed into a school discussion on access for older people and disabled to schools, other build- ings, and to transport services. The children were prepared for some of the physical difficulties they would encounter, and developed communication skills which would help them on their visits: speaking clearly, making eye contact and using touch.

The first visit took place on a warm summer's day. The children set up a maypole on an old tennis court at the hospital and the residents, some in wheelchairs, sat in the shade of the trees to watch. Maypole dancing, and music and singing that everyone could join in, followed. The children began to intro- duce themselves to the patients and the ice was gradually broken. Two old ladies were so moved by the children's performance that they began to cry – a reaction which the children found difficult to understand at first. Games on the grass followed and after ninety minutes the patients were left looking forward to the children's next visit.

Two further visits followed, one out-of-doors and one in the hospital's arts studio where children worked in pairs with a patient using clay to make models. Some patients preferred to watch but some who were initially reluctant were eventually enthused by the children to such an extent that they joined in.

Evaluating the project, LinkAge concluded that both sides of the link had enjoyed it and wanted it to continue. The weekly sessions went on successfully for nearly a year and covered a wide range of activities (see Figures 6, 7, and 8).

By the end of the year everyone involved felt that a great deal had been gained, sometimes in surprising ways. The class teacher was originally interested in the project as a stimulus to classroom work and was prepared to end it as soon as interest waned. However, this did not happen, to quote him:

It has been splendid and has worked on so many levels that I didn't imagine. Working in a different and sometimes difficult

Figure 7 *Patients from Bethnal Green Hospital and pupils from St John's School found great pleasure and stimulation from each other's company. (Photograph by Jacky Chapman; used by courtesy of the* Times Educational Supplement *and* LinkAge)

Figure 8   *Pupils and patients worked together to make decorations, invitations, hats and cakes for their joint Christmas party at the hospital. (Photograph by Jacky Chapman; used by courtesy of the Times Educational Supplement and LinkAge)*

environment with people of a different generation I have seen a side to the children that they rarely have the chance to demonstrate in school. I have seen them grow in self-confidence, esteem and improved communication skills that they now put to use in other contexts.

Some children established firm 'special relationships' with older patients. Amongst both groups there were individuals who found it relatively hard to communicate. This difficulty was overcome to some extent by setting up small groups to work together which included 'non-talkers' of both ages. At the hospital, efforts were made to publicize the scheme and carry it over into everyday life with the help of photographs, displays, etc. In school, six children wrote up each visit for a class diary and put on an assembly to explain to the rest of the school what they were doing.

The school–hospital team had to confront the situation which would arise if one of the children's special friends should die. In the second term of the project one of the popular patients involved died only a day after three children had made a special visit to her bedside to show her the Hallowe'en masks they were making. The children were told in school a few days later and every attempt was made to answer their questions and help them to come to terms with an event which saddened them greatly. The hospital passed on the patient's Pink Panther toy to the children, and this was kept in the classroom as a reminder of her. The toy became a fixture in the classroom and the children talked about their friend for some time. Though there were some tears, the visits to the hospital were not affected.

Tower Hamlets College

Six students from the photography and video course spent several weeks documenting the sessions at the hospital. This was a challenging brief in which they had to overcome many technical difficulties such as poor lighting, working with several groupings in a large area, and trying to capture intimate moments without being obtrusive. They quickly became involved and often stayed to talk to the patients once the children had returned to school.

The result was a video film and an exhibition of photographs of a surprisingly high standard.

The original links with the hospital ended with the closure of the hospital and a 'home-warming party' at the new Bancroft Unit at the London Hospital to which the patients transferred. The party enabled the children to see where their friends had gone and gave a chance for proper leave-taking.

New links were established with other schools near by. A class from *Guardian Angels Primary School* started their project by cultivating plants from seed in the classroom and then worked with the patients to plant them out in the raised flower-beds outside their wards. Pupils from *Raines Foundation School* had already visited the Bethnal Green Hospital for school project work and then became involved in LinkAge sessions. Two pupils made a LinkAge suggestion box for the school, which was fed with ideas for activities and fund-raising. The LinkAge worker met with a large group of enthusiastic pupils to discuss their well-thought-out suggestions.

Some were impossible because of school timetable restrictions and to date the weekly visits are taking place out of school hours. Some ideas they plan to pursue are:

- an after-school club with board games and refreshments;
- to help patients with personal grooming: manicure, hair and make-up;
- exercise classes for wheelchair-bound patients;
- to design and make board games for patients who are visually impaired.

LinkAge workers in Tower Hamlets report that local reaction to the project has been almost universally positive. Professionals in education and social services offered support and encouragement as did Age Concern locally and the management at Bethnal Green Hospital.

The working model for LinkAge projects remains unchanged, with activities which are mutually rewarding for both generations and the careful preparation of children in advance of their visits. They are now helped by the hospital's occupational and speech therapists. These two departments were initially encouraged to work with LinkAge when nursing staff noted the extent to which patients were motivated to overcome difficulties in speech and mobility in order to join in activities with visiting children.

Gracemount Primary School, Lothian

As part of the Young and Old Together initiative in Lothian, this primary school introduced a project on older people and ageing to its junior pupils. The project began through personal contact between a teacher at the school and a nurse at Southfield Hospital, the local geriatric hospital. They set out four objectives for the scheme: to establish the children's attitudes towards growing old and being old; to make a record of their ideas and feelings both before and after the project; to give the old people and children the chance to meet and enjoy each other's company; and to let the older people share the children's experiences at school through conversation and a video made in school.

Part of the project involved asking the children to write poems based on their impressions of old age before and after a series of visits to, and contacts with, older people in the local community. The first three poems reflect a *before* view of age, the next three a changed perspective *after* relationships had been built up.

Growing old

You get grey hair.

Wrinkles start to creep.

And you can't quite make the stair.

Your teeth are not always your own.

You feel the cold.

So this is growing old.

            Donald

Being old is:

Having wrinkles on your body.

You walk slowly.

You get weaker.
You get grey hairs.
You get skinnier.
You get colder easily.
You lose your sight.
You hurt easily.
You don't eat much.
You don't exercise
and you wear warmer clothes.

Claire

Being old is:
having old things,
staying in the house,
teeth go black,
hair goes yellow,
Old things go rusty,
Old things go yellow.

Greig

Growing old
Growing old is a funny thing,
Still going like a spring,
In the morning is a cup of tea,
Then going sailing out to sea.
Old people can still float
Just like a little boat.
Some old people have walking sticks,
Some old people do gymnastics.

Paul

Growing old is fun,
It's not just down in the dumps,
You can jump in the air,
Clap your hands,
Ride a bike,
Fly a kite.
Growing old is fun.

Kirsty

Growing Old
Growing old is remembering
Old times, and comparing them with new ones.
It is sometimes sad and sometimes fun.
Some old people do things like us
And sometimes make a little fuss.
Some run about and always count
How many press-ups they can do!

Donald

The children made several visits to the hospital and joined in a patient's birthday party on one occasion. The reaction of the hospital staff to the project was enthusiastic:

It was very good. The children seem to have enjoyed this as much as the old folk did. It has given them a kinder idea of old age.

It quite made Pie and Cissy's morning when I told them what the children had said about them. I was very impressed by the amount of work the children had done and the fact that they would seem to have enjoyed the visits as much as the patients have enjoyed them coming here.

PROVIDING SERVICES FOR OLDER PEOPLE

Marlborough School, Woodstock

This comprehensive school has been involved in activities with older people in the town and the surrounding villages for the last six years. A community service scheme for pupils offers help to older people in the area, especially to the house-bound. Pupils have undertaken shopping, gardening, decorating, cleaning and regular collection of pensions for the 'clients'.

At Christmas the school presented a concert for older people and provided transport to bring members of the audience in from surrounding villages. The school organized a fun-run, with 600 runners in fancy dress, to raise funds for a Christmas dinner for pensioners. Sixth-formers served the meal and provided an after-lunch entertainment. Some of the older guests had not been able to visit the town of Woodstock for years because of ill-health or disability, and some met friends they had not seen for twenty years.

ARTS-BASED PROJECTS

Behind Wise Eyes – the West Dorset arts in education project

This was a project organized by South West Arts (SWA) and funded by BP and the Gulbenkian Foundation, with some help from SWA, Dorset Education Authority and the Dorset Arts Development Fund. The aim was twofold: to enable school-children to work with practising artists in school time – in this case with the objective of producing their own books – and to extend previous oral history work into a project which would bring old and young together in a way that would encourage children to explore their perceptions and interpretations of old age.

The project brought together 125 children from three Dorset middle schools, four artists – a writer, calligrapher, print-maker and book-binder – and residents of a geriatric ward at West Dorset District Hospital. It was regarded by SWA as a pilot, upon which other individuals and institutions could build within the limits and constraints of their own personnel and resources. For this reason, SWA has published a booklet and a video about the project, which detail how Behind Wise Eyes was set up and evaluate how successful it was over the five-month period in 1989 during which it ran.

In the context of this book it is valuable to look at some of the reactions of those who took part in the project to the element of intergenerational contact. The first objective was to introduce groups of children to older hospital-bound people who were willing and able to meet them and to talk about their lives and experiences. This was not always an easy thing for either side to do. In spite of preparation for the initial visits to the hospital ward, children found that some of their conversational initiatives soon dried up, and that older people also found it difficult sometimes to communicate as freely as they might wish.

Because the children had a specific academic objective to their visits – to collect material for their books – there were constraints which would not have been apparent in a more open-ended project. For instance, they used tape recorders to record their conversations and this must have been inhibiting to both sides. Even so, valuable relationships were built up, as comments from teachers and hospital staff evaluating the project indicate.

Older people themselves, although some found speech itself a struggle because of their medical conditions, welcomed the new intervention into their highly circumscribed lives in which children and young people no longer, on the whole, played any part. One old man had gained great pleasure from talking about his days as a shepherd. Marjorie, who had only one visitor a week normally and found her time on the ward dragged, especially at weekends, commented: 'I like it when you come here. You make me feel human again.'

The children themselves had been deeply moved by the experience. As one put it:

> There seemed to be invisible barriers around each of them and
> that's what makes me act friendly towards them. They don't look
> as if they're with today's world, and sometimes I wish I could
> know what's going on in their heads because I'd find it impossible

to sit all day and not think about anything. Somehow I always feel they're sad about today's goings on.

By the end of their visits, when close relationships had built up, another child wrote:

Even though Marjorie says she missed us week after week, I missed her too. I enjoyed her company and could have lived in the hospital with her.

According to the ward staff who evaluated the project after it was finished, the main value to the older patients was psychological. 'The older ones all brightened up and were very interested in the visits.' The consultant physician concluded that he would like to see visits continue on a regular basis.

In the schools, there was considerable variation in teachers' reactions to the project. One English teacher commented that his children had been enthused by the artistic input to the project but had not found the subject of old age a particularly stimulating one. Another reported that there had been some negative comments on the hospital visits from some children.

Another teacher was much more positive:

I felt I wanted to be part of this project to encourage the boys and girls to be aware that old age does not necessarily mean illness, weakness and numbness of emotions. I think they have experienced this. I think they have developed an empathy for their older friends through the exchange of thoughts and ideas. That their sensitivity has been heightened by this experience is evident from the apparent ease that they progressively accepted the tasks we have asked of them.

The full report of the Behind Wise Eyes project is invaluable in that it does not gloss over the difficulties which may arise in bringing together schoolchildren and the more frail or handicapped elderly people in hospitals and homes. Communication is not necessarily easy in these circumstances, and to be successful projects will need the same amount of careful planning and evaluation – fully reported – that went into the Dorset scheme.

MAGIC ME IN LONDON

'Magic Me' was started in the United States in 1981 by Kathy Levin. She had been shocked by the isolation of older people in a nursing home she had visited and launched a scheme which aimed to bring the energy and enthusiasm of children to bear on some of the problems of residential care. Magic Me projects are now running in forty American states.

The project came to London in 1988 when three pilot schemes were launched in Tower Hamlets, Islington and Westminster, each linking a primary school to an old people's home. Magic Me (UK) was formed in 1989 and attention is now being focused mainly on the borough of Tower Hamlets.

The core of the Magic Me approach is a weekly visit by children to a nearby residential home. Before the first visit is made, children take part in training sessions at school at which they are encouraged to talk about their attitudes to, and fears about, old age and to consider issues of ageing, disability, responsibility and interdependence. They take part in role-play to discover how it might feel to be deaf, or blind or immobile, and they are prepared for the experience, sometimes shocking or unpleasant, of their first visit.

The visits are led by a Magic Me project worker and focus on a range of arts projects including photography, dance, music and the visual arts. Each activity is designed to stimulate all the participants, old and young alike. The emphasis is on the individual contribution of the child, who is encouraged to use his or her unique personality, skills and enthusiasm in the relationships which are going to be built up. Sessions are often linked to work in the children's classroom.

There is careful follow-up of the visits. Children are encouraged in discussion to talk about their reactions to the visits, to raise any problems, and to work out solutions to them. In some circumstances children can be remarkably persistent. In one residential home an older man who had a stroke and was frustrated by his inability to speak watched every session for six months but left the room as soon as anyone tried to engage him in conversation. Gradually the children made friends with him and persuaded him to write down the words they could not understand

Figure 9   *Magic Me projects bring the energy and enthusiasm of children into the lives of older people in residential care. (Photograph by Susan Langford; used by courtesy of Magic Me)*

when he spoke. He went on to take part in drawing and clay-modelling sessions.

The projects are also evaluated by residents and staff at the homes and hospitals. By regularly monitoring what is going on during the visits, and residents' and children's reactions to them, care staff can become more involved and help to plan future developments in co-operation with the schools and project workers.

Magic Me has now drawn up a three-year plan to develop beyond Tower Hamlets. This takes on board all the changes in educational and health provision which have either begun or are likely to begin over the period. It will in future include secondary school children and residents of sheltered accommodation, and has widened the range of artistic activities which are offered.

MAGIC ME AT REDLANDS PRIMARY SCHOOL

Redlands is a multiracial primary school in Tower Hamlets. More than 90 per cent of its pupils are of Bangladeshi origin. The project took place at a time when school staffing in the borough was particularly difficult. That fact, and a fear that the school's children might meet some racism at an old people's home where all the residents were white and some were Jewish, was thoroughly discussed by the staff at the school and the home before the project started. In the event there were no problems and all the residents responded to the visiting children in a very positive way.

Ten children were chosen to take part in the visits although the school hoped to include most of the sixty fourth-year (10-year-old) pupils over time. The children took part in two training sessions before their first visit. Questions raised included:

- Why do we have old people's homes?
- What does it mean to be lonely?
- What is our image of an old person?
- What is a residential home like?
- What is the job of the care staff?

- What is the worst thing that could happen there?
- How can we make a difference to the lives of the people there?
- What happens if someone doesn't want us there?

A few children had experience of living with an older relative while others found it hard to move away from their image of 'sweet old ladies'.

The children needed help and support on their first visit to introduce themselves to the residents. They found talking loudly enough to be heard by the hard-of-hearing difficult. They had to learn to communicate by writing or lip-reading with two deaf residents. However, the ice was broken and photographs were taken as a useful tool for follow-up work in school and to break the ice on the second visit.

After several visits individual friendships were developing between the two generations and shared art-based activities provided a focus which retained the children's interest and provided a stimulus for conversation. The best results were achieved in one-to-one activities with the children encouraging and helping a resident to complete an activity or to try something new. Activities ranged from drawings based on reminiscences or fantasies, to clay model-making, painting, sweet-making, and hand-jiving (see Figure 10).

It was clear at the end of the project that the vast majority of older people had enjoyed the visits. They looked forward to the weekly event and its associated activities, and even some who were reluctant to join in were happy to watch. The activities allowed them to be creative and to think imaginatively.

The children grew in confidence as the project progressed and enjoyed using their energy and skills with the old people. Shy children found that adults were themselves sometimes lacking in confidence, and the more boisterous learned to slow down and adapt their behaviour to the pace of the residents.

Comments from participants show the powerful effect of Magic Me on the lives of some of the people involved.

> Friday without Magic Me could not exist. There is an actual physical lift when the children come. It is as if there is no generational gap between the children and the residents. I only wish I had Magic Me and the kids on my other two floors.
> (*Assistant manager of a residential home*)

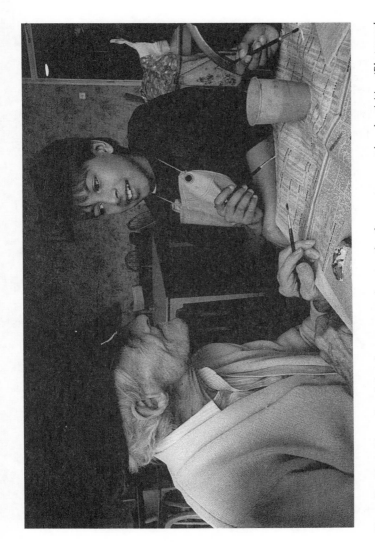

Figure 10 *Magic Me projects bring the two generations together for one-to-one art-based activities. (Photograph by Richard Madden; used by courtesy of Magic Me)*

You and the children. You're the only ones I know. The only ones I remember.
(*Older resident*)

They're jolly, liven the place up.
(*Older resident*)

They are learning how to approach older people, learning to accept. Usually children would be frightened and with the residents would be patronizing and 'sympathetic'. But in Magic Me sessions they are not like that.
(*Headteacher*)

In Magic Me I have learnt that not all old people are kind. Some are nice, others are grumpy. Just like everybody else.
(*Pupil*)

Chapter 4

Oral History and Reminiscence

Geriatric hospitals and homes for older people have for a number of years been developing reminiscence with their patients as a therapy. The objective is to encourage older people – often with the help of photographs and objects from the past – to recall their own life histories and so become more communicative. The Help the Aged newsletter, *Recall*, told a remarkable story about a project organized for a group of mentally handicapped older people in Mansfield which included 'Fred', who as far as anyone knew could neither read, write, nor speak.

> For months he looked at many books with only mild interest. For a six-week period we had a young man on attachment from the Prince of Wales Trust who took in a book on boxing. Suddenly noises emanated from Fred and after much pushing he started to write messages to Matthew. It turned out Fred had been a boxer and so Matthew did a special research project using pictures and books for the period of his boxing career. Fred became one of the most dedicated members of the project and from the man who 'couldn't write' came messages and information.

The library in Mansfield was involved in that project at the request of the social services department. They began by taking artefacts and photographs out to old people's homes and have since devised a pack of materials which is available to anyone in the area who wants to organize reminiscence activities. It consists of packs of photographs, quizzes, song-sheets, tapes, histories of local industry, ideas for speakers, and sample readings/

Figure 11   *Local history was brought alive for pupils from Bishop's Road Primary School when they interviewed elderly local residents during a LinkAge project in Bristol.*

monologues. This is backed up by a collection of items which can be borrowed on a short-term basis: videos, tapes, books, etc. The library has also been involved in training staff from local homes for older people.

In 1989 the library organized a three-week exhibition and series of events which included local materials, diaries, a 'senses booth' (which allowed people to remember old-style remedies and ointments by sight or smell), and a great deal of material lent by older residents of the town.

This sort of project does not necessarily involve young people, although it is significant that the person who got through to Fred in the Mansfield home was a young volunteer. But the community of interest between older people, who gain from reminiscence, and the young, who are studying local history, is obvious. Many schools have begun to explore history with the help of older people in their communities.

For those wishing to launch oral history and reminiscence projects, Maureen Farquharson of Arran High School, whose project is described in detail later in this chapter, says that there are four main considerations:

1. Older people have to be convinced that they have something of value to offer to the younger generation – and some have to be persuaded to venture into the school.
2. The school has to consider practical ways in which it can become a more integral part of local life – the project itself raises problems of community liaison, transport, timetabling, and teamwork for a staff who are seldom natives of the community.
3. The work has to be developed and assessed as a meaningful course for the pupil.
4. Ideally the arts should offer a community the opportunity to express its own culture in music, drama and painting. Only then can old traditions and values be appreciated as being relevant today.

Maureen Farquharson argues that there are two aspects of the local culture which are of especial value to the island of Arran's modern schoolchildren: the collective knowledge about a way of life which goes back centuries, and the quality of human relationships which have always been an essential part of the Gaelic society which is now fading. Older people of Arran, she says, can pass on the skills upon which the survival of their traditional society depended, their skills in the natural environment, and their skills in the social environment. Her school's gatherings between old and young are a direct descendant, she thinks, of the ceilidh through which traditional Gaelic society passed on its customs, values, and folk-lore for centuries.

The gap between an old culture now fading and modern life is not perhaps quite so deep in other parts of the United Kingdom, but is in most places a real one, which can to some extent be bridged by oral history and reminiscence projects.

LOANHEAD PRIMARY SCHOOL, LOTHIAN

During Celebrating Age Week in 1988, Loanhead Primary School decided to extend the work that was already going on there with residents from a local old people's home, who had been involved very successfully in one-to-one reading with children. Class P3 (7-year-olds) were about to start a project on 'Our School' and it was decided to incorporate discussions with the older people into the project. As assistant head, Maureen Crandles, wrote in the *Times Educational Supplement*, it was hoped that this would be a two-way process, enabling the children to find out about schooling in their grandparents' time and older people to learn something about modern education.

On the Thursday of Celebrating Age Week, grandparents were invited to accompany their grandchildren to school: thirty turned up, including two great-grandmothers and one great-grandfather. They sat together and followed the normal morning's timetable, including some 'messy' play. At playtime, parents served the grandparents with tea and biscuits.

For the afternoon session, a 1937 classroom had been set up with the help of the History of Education Centre in Edinburgh, complete with slates, inkwells, and double wooden desks. The children and teachers dressed in period clothes and spent the afternoon chanting tables, taking dictation, and doing drill – old and young alike.

Discussion followed, with the grandparents admitting that the younger generation were more independent and confident when learning than they had been, and the youngsters confessing to an attachment to double desks which could be shared with a friend.

WHITECROSS SCHOOL REMEDIAL UNIT, LYDNEY, GLOUCESTERSHIRE

In the early 1980s this comprehensive school was organized with a special unit on site for disruptive and slow-learning youngsters. The unit had effective control of its own timetable and involved its young people in community work with older people: the usual round of visits to do decorating, gardening, etc. To foster relationships between the generations – and in response to a challenge from Help the Aged to find ways of strengthening links – it was decided to invite older residents into school as well, purely for a social visit. One conversation led to another and it soon became clear that older visitors were a source of fascinating local information which caught the imagination of many of the 'difficult' children in the unit. Staff decided that there was the basis there for a more formal local history project involving the two generations. What followed was unusual in that it was based entirely on the remedial unit, where children less articulate and less confident than most were encouraged to undertake a major intergenerational project.

Soon after it became clear that interesting aspects of local history were emerging from the children's contacts, staff wrote a series of articles for the local newspaper which brought in many more offers of help and information. Publicity, the school felt, also boosted the pupils' confidence in what they were doing. The trickle of information soon became a flood, with old photographs, scrapbooks and memorabilia of all sorts being sent or brought to the school.

The school decided that it had stumbled upon a valuable resource which could be used both by pupils across a range of subjects and by the local community. The local Heritage Museum was asked if it could house the artefacts which had been collected and make use of the videotapes the children had made of some of their older friends' reminiscences.

The school then produced a small booklet entitled *Forest Memories*, containing some of the videotaped material. This led to increased interest in the local community, more contributions, and a professionally produced version of the book. A second volume, entitled *Tinplaters of Lydney and Lydbrook*, was produced, being funded by a loan of £500 from the town council and by local industrialists. Both books sold well, enabling the school to repay its debts within two years.

An award from the Schools Curriculum Development Committee allowed the project to develop even further as pupils began to excavate a seventeenth-century iron furnace in the school grounds – an enterprise which brought in more older visitors offering information and help. This resulted in a third publication.

The Whitecross project came to an end when the special unit children were reintegrated into the mainstream of the school in the late 1980s. But its influence continues in the scheme of community work which is now available to all fourth- and fifth-year pupils and which includes work for and with older people.

LINKAGE PROJECTS

In many projects where LinkAge brings the generations together, reminiscence is an incidental but important part of their shared activities. In other cases, oral history is the focus and has been explored in a variety of ways, as shown in the three examples that follow.

Bishop's Road Primary School, Bristol

Third- and fourth-year pupils were involved in a LinkAge pilot project with members of the Bishopston Church Fellowship Group in the summer of 1989. Groups of three or four children interviewed one or two senior citizens about their memories of the war in Bristol. The result was a project book which recorded the interviews and included photographs and drawings of life during the Second World War. The project brought out much incidental information about life in the 1930s and 1940s – wash-days, rationing, gas masks and air-raid shelters, where bombs fell locally (one in the school playground!), children's games, changes in diet, etc. Pride of place in the project book goes to a drawing of medals and their ribbons 'by Emily Bowie's grandad' (see Figure 12).

Oxford

In a joint venture with the County Council's Museums Service, LinkAge is producing a collection of Reminiscence Boxes. These are thematic and contain artefacts and photographs. They will have a number of uses, including bringing older and younger people together on creative writing projects stimulated by discussion on the themes.

Tower Hamlets

A LinkAge older volunteer with a wealth of memories had a regular placement at the Children's Library to help visiting schools with local history projects.

ST FRANCIS FIRST SCHOOL, OXFORD

Initiatives involving old people at this small Church of England first (5–9) school on the southern edge of Oxford sprang from a Community Education development project which had temporary funding for two years up to November 1990. The brief of the development officer was to look at a small suburban 'patch' of mixed private and council housing, with a population of about 5,000 and few community facilities. The major institutions in the area were the first school and an old people's home, Shotover View.

A long-term reminiscence project had been started at Shotover View in which the memories of old people were being recorded and illustrated by a community education out-reach worker and care assistant. Children from St Francis were invited to take part in this project and have visited on a regular basis. The children's work after the first year of visits culminated in an exhibition of

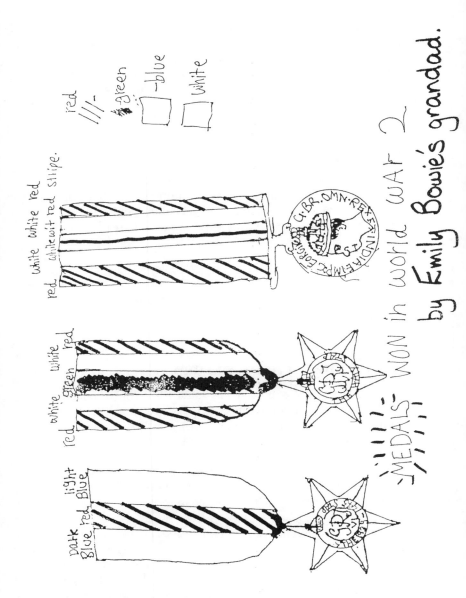

Figure 12 *A LinkAge project book of wartime memories based on interviews with members of the Bishopston Church Fellowship group was compiled and illustrated by the pupils of Bishop's Road Primary School.*

writing and drawing on the old people's memories of their childhood and the area. In the second year, older people have helped to make work-cards for the children to use in school. These include drawings of many of the residents of the home, which are on display in the school and provide a moving record of the children's relationships with their 'neighbours' in the home. Teaching staff at St Francis are enthusiastic about the educational and personal benefits which have flowed from the relationship between the school and the home. They say that the children have gained a new understanding about older people and old age and death. The old people's pleasure at the children's visits is obvious.

PEERS SCHOOL, OXFORD

Talking about the past is part of the formal and informal curriculum at this comprehensive school. Students studying 'Conflict' as part of their GCSE integrated Humanities course are required to research how the Second World War affected people's lives in Britain. This involves using written sources, such as newspapers and magazines, as well as talking to relatives, neighbours and friends who experienced the war at first hand. Interviews have been conducted at old people's homes and in sheltered accommodation in the city.

Similar visits were made by children at the school as part of their Activities Week, which included an option on life during the Second World War entitled 'We'll meet again'. Pupils visited Cutteslowe Court Old People's Home and discussed wartime experiences, including being evacuated, having evacuees at home, the fear of bombing, and the victory celebrations.

WHEN WE WERE YOUNG: SOUTH SOMERSET

This was a major project involving the Age Exchange Theatre Trust; South Somerset District Council Leisure and Arts Department; and Take Art!, a rural arts agency. It also received financial backing from Somerset County Council (the local education authority), from South West Arts, and from shoe manufacturers C. and J. Clark – a major employer in the area.

The project aimed to encourage people in what could be isolated rural communities to become involved in recreational activities, and also to bring the older and younger generations together. A number of communities expressed an interest in taking part in a reminiscence project and, after seeing the Age Exchange exhibition 'What Did You Do in the War, Mum?', five decided to work over a period of months on the theme 'When we were young'.

In three of the villages close working relationships were built up between a school and an old people's home. The children produced art, drama, and written work stimulated by the memories of older people they made contact with. These comments from children at Swanmead Community Middle School, Ilminster, give some idea of the children's own reactions to their drama project based on memories of the Second World War.

> It started as fun and finished with us intrigued. We'd never gone so deep into anything like this before. It was us who wanted to know, and by asking the experts we found out. The experts at first made us nervous. Now they're our friends. They've helped us and we hope we've given them our friendship and trust. I hope they feel the play is as much theirs as ours.
> (*Emma Dean*)

> I think that I've got a better understanding about the Second World War. I used to think that there were only tears in families when someone from their family had been sent off to fight the war . . . I know now that in the olden days children were more close to their grandparents and that the grandmother, when her husband died or got sent to fight the war, usually moved in with her eldest son.
> (*Sarah Scribbins*)

The project culminated with a 'When We Were Young' Festival of Reminiscence, held on a perfect summer's day in July 1990 in the idyllic setting of Dillington House, Somerset County Council's in-service education centre. The festival included an exhibition of old photographs and artefacts from the area, a tea-dance, three live performances by children and young people based on reminiscences, and the launch of the Age Exchange book to celebrate the project, also entitled *When We Were Young*.

Commenting on the success of the South Somerset project, Pam Schweitzer, artistic director of Age Exchange, wrote in *When We Were Young*:

> One of the merits of this project is that it has drawn in many people who had not previously experienced the pleasure of working closely on their memories with a group of older people and making something lasting of them. This collaborative work is demanding for staff who are often already hard-pressed in the work they are doing in residential homes and day centres but they have found it to be stimulating and enlightening.
>
> For the old people themselves it has been fun, a challenge, a chance to make new relationships and try new activities and, most significantly, a means of dramatically improving their own self-image.
>
> Some of the most special relationships to have emerged from this project have been those between schoolchildren and older people . . . Teachers and residential workers have noted the enjoyment derived by children and old people from this contact. It has had a most positive effect on young people's thinking about older people in their area. This is likely to have a lasting effect on their attitudes in later life, and there are plans to continue this cross-generational work after the project has finished.

ARRAN HIGH SCHOOL HERITAGE PROJECT

The island of Arran, off Scotland's west coast but close enough to the major centres of population to be part of its most populous local authority, Strathclyde, might seem a place where an older idea of 'community' could have survived better than it has in the cities. In fact the culture of the island is changing. It is now five generations since the clearances destroyed the traditional farming culture. More than half the pupils at the island's small high school come from families which have moved there either from mainland Scotland or from as far away as Yorkshire: holidaymakers who have returned to live. The Gaelic language has fallen into disuse, and, according to Maureen Farquharson who has developed the school's Heritage Project, there is a gulf between many of the children on the island and the older generation.

The Heritage Project, which is now in its tenth year at the school, is intended to use the reminiscences of the island's older people as a stimulus to a creative relationship between the two generations. In 1990 the project started before Christmas (a little earlier than in previous years). It involves second-year pupils (13- and 14-year-olds) and culminates in a display of work to which everyone on the island is invited.

Maureen Farquharson says that the first problem is to persuade the islanders that they have something of value to give to the children. Contact is made in all the small island communities with the help of community councillors, retired doctors and ministers, and anyone else who knows the community well. This is especially valuable as only one of the teachers involved in the project is an islander. An incidental benefit for older people is that the gatherings often bring together older residents from remote parts of the island who have not seen each other for many years.

The project proper starts with a 'gathering' at which the pupils and older people meet each other and the pupils arrange a 'home interview' which will be the main basis for a piece of illustrated written work based on the older person's reminiscences. It can be augmented by drawings, photographs, etc., and the school staff lend support and advice. For instance, Science staff may look at Gaelic ballads and music, Geography and Art may work together on traditional methods of agriculture. 'Pairs' of young and older people are carefully matched by staff, and tape recorders are used to record conversations.

As far as the pupil is concerned, the school starts from where they are – where their family came from; where they live now on the island; the history of the house, the street or farm and village. The focus gradually becomes wider as the child's own interests develop, and specific skills are needed – for instance, the study of artefacts on museum visits, map-work, the reading of archival material, etc.

The inspiration for the project was the Orkney St Magnus Festival, which celebrates Orkney life in music, poetry and drama once a year. Maureen Farquharson took a group of Arran children there in 1980 and out of that experience grew the seeds of the project at the High School which still continues.

The project ends each year with the production of a 'book' of the children's reminiscence work and a display of work at the school, to which the community is invited. The book is added to the school library's growing collection of books on the island and on Scottish history.

Summing up the benefits of the project, Mrs Farquharson says that the project is building up a special kind of relationship between Arran High School and the community, and between the older and younger generation. The older inhabitants of the island are experiencing a sense of contributing to the education of the younger generation by handing on their knowledge of the island – knowledge which might otherwise be lost. The teachers who take part, many of them newcomers to the island, benefit by working on a cross-curricular and multi-media project and acquire an insight into the traditions of Arran. The pupils learn new skills and learn how to identify with and contribute to their own community. And the project is helping to preserve the cultural heritage of Arran and also beginning to stimulate ways of reinvigorating that culture.

Perhaps the last word on the Arran Heritage Project should be left to some of the young people who have taken part.

My great grandpa, Bob Currie, used to be the blacksmith at Rosaburn. It was built in 1777 and closed down in 1965. It is now part of the Arran Heritage Museum.

In the 1920s and 1930s Bob employed several men as there was lots of work for blacksmiths then. In the summer months the trade would double. They hired out carriages for the summer visitors and three horses for farm work. All the materials for the smiddy came from P. and R. Fleming, Glasgow. To shoe a horse for all four feet cost 10d. To put on an old shoe on one foot cost 1d.

Bob's day started at 6 a.m. and finished at 6 p.m. During the winter some of the older men would gather round the fire and help to keep the three fires going. The smiddy used to be the meeting place for the whole village.

(*Graham Dobson*)

I was talking to John Mc. and there was this story he told me about a man called Sandy who lived long ago in a cottage near my council house. Sandy had one cow, one field and one haystack. Well, he did not like his mother-in-law very much. Sandy felt that his wife and his mother-in-law spent too much time clacking at the gate when she went up and down the road to Lagg. So one summer to spite her he built his one haystack in front of the kitchen window so that his wife could not see her mother coming.

My great-great-great-grandfather lived on the Holy Isle. He had twelve children who all grew up and went away. Except young Janet. But one dark and stormy night a large schooner named the *Mary Anne* from Ireland was almost shipwrecked near Lamlash. Her crew and the captain, James Teare, had to take shelter on the Holy Isle. There he met and fell in love with Janet. They eloped. They married on the Isle of McGee in Ireland – and they had fourteen children.

REMEMBERING THE SECOND WORLD WAR: AGE EXCHANGE THEATRE TRUST

In 1990 a typical event organized by the London-based charity Age Exchange took place at the Woolwich Railway Museum, a small and elegant disused station on the north bank of the Thames which houses a collection of railway memorabilia and some engines and carriages. Children who had been studying the Second World War in local schools were invited to 'be evacuated' from the station. Actors and actresses in 1930s costume – some professionals and others amateurs – served as the teachers and officials escorting a London school class to a train to the country. Gas masks were handed out; 'luggage', some of it done up in pillow-cases, had been provided; and the children were marshalled at the station and shepherded aboard just as they would have been in 1939 (see Figure 13).

Older volunteers who had themselves been evacuated from just such a platform fifty years ago were on hand to spend time with the children answering questions and describing exactly what the experience had been like. One railway carriage was given over to an exhibition of work by children who had attended a whole-day Theatre in Education programme at Age Exchange's Reminiscence Centre on the subject of evacuation, and this exhibition by other pupils gave an added freshness to the experience.

It was clear from talking to both young and old who took part that the experience was a very positive one for both generations. The event had arisen out of a major project on evacuation by Age Exchange which was funded by the Inner London Education Authority; entitled 'Good-night Children Everywhere', it marked the fiftieth anniversary of the massive exodus of children from

Figure 13 *Age Exchange brought together schoolchildren, actors, and older people who were wartime evacuees, to relive the experience at a railway museum. (Photograph by Alex Schweizer; used by courtesy of Age Exchange)*

London. This brought together professional actors, school-children and older people to work creatively on a drama production based on evacuation reminiscences. Whole classes of children worked in a specially prepared three-dimensional exhibition environment, which featured actual artefacts and letters from the time, as a basis for Theatre in Education work.

On a chilly day in Woolwich, children showed obvious enthusiasm for the project, and volunteers had no doubt of the happiness they had gained through working constructively with the younger generation.

> I get a great deal of satisfaction from this. It gives me a real inner glow. Last week I went to the school to talk to the children who are here today. I had a ration-book, a gas mask and an identity card. It was amazing what they didn't know. They didn't know what a searchlight was, or how all the railings were taken down during the war. Their teacher said that this was a class you couldn't talk to, but their faces lighted up with interest. I go to the Centre on Fridays and Saturdays and I spent two hours once talking to a 13-year-old about the war.
> (*Margaret Phair*)

> I have been working as a volunteer at the Centre and I have been out to schools to talk about the war years. The reaction of the children is wonderful. There was not enough time in an hour and a half for all their questions and I had to leave the toys I had taken with me behind.
> (*Irene Swanton*)

> I still get upset about being evacuated when I was 9. It was a very intense experience and I think working through it again has done me good. I still have all the letters I wrote when I was an evacuee [see Figure 14]. My mother had kept them. I think it is very interesting for the children here.
> (*Joan Herring*)

> Seeing the war through the eyes of these wartime evacuees has enabled today's children to make far more sense of those years than they might have achieved from the average history lesson. This meeting across the generations has been creative and productive for both age groups and the original evacuees have been happy to see their experience put to good use. They have all found that the task of telling, writing down or tape-recording their experiences was worth while, partly so that their experience of that difficult period could be more widely understood by others, and partly for their own peace of mind.
> (*Pam Schweitzer, artistic director, Age Exchange*)

Joan Herring in Worthing.

1

37, Lincoln Rd,
Torring,
West Worthing

Dear Mum e Dad, I hope you are
keeping well. You know I said
that the money I had would
last me a month? Well I
have only sixpence left. It
was the pictures that did it
they cost eightpence. I would
like you to bring me the
Worlds Greatest Wonders please
(not the Wonders of the
World). I wrote to Auntie Vic
and she replied yesterday.
I want Mrs Corns Husband
to come home he is a Petty
Officer on the H.M.S. "Hood"
and he has three stripes.

Letters from Joan to her mother.

2

Is dad working in Victoria Station? If he is he can couze home to dinner cant he? I am jud munching one of my chocolates they are lovely. The ribbin on the lid is in peices but I can take the bow of and put it on a clip. Please exuse the writing I know it is terrible but you know what I am for writing.

We are knitting 6" squares to join to gether and make into blankets for the reff-ugees. Miss Fanny Fuss Face Jackson has found us a hall and we have to walk a hundred miles to it It is a terrible long way to go, Isn't it terrible

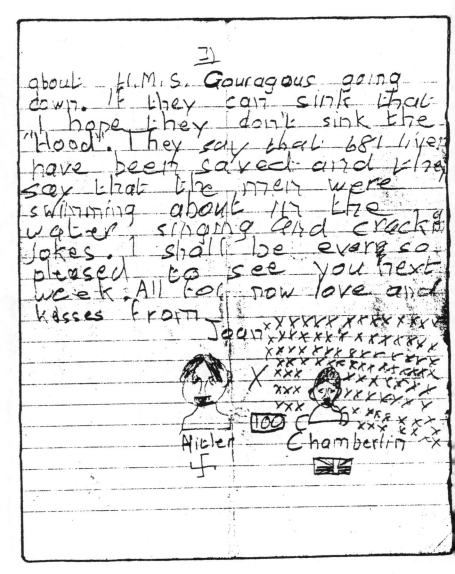

Figure 14 *An original letter from Joan Herring to her parents was one of many contributions from older people who shared their memories of evacuation for an Age Exchange project 'Good-night Children Everywhere'.*

SIGHTHILL COMMUNITY CENTRE, EDINBURGH

Intergenerational projects linking Sighthill Community Education Centre and local primary schools have been going on for the past nine years. These have brought together older people attending the luncheon club at the community centre with older primary children (aged 10 and 11) in historical work which has incorporated older residents' reminiscences of the local area and of national events.

Children at Murrayburn Primary School undertook a major project on 'How we used to live, 1900–1926' between November 1986 and February 1987. The project was cross-curricular, involving children in history, literature, drama, and role-play. It ranged from the struggle for women's suffrage, through the battles of the First World War, to fashion and culture in the 1920s. The project was fully documented by the senior community education worker at Sighthill, Sheila Brown, and her reports give an interesting insight into the careful preparatory and follow-up work which she came to regard as essential to the success of this project.

The children spent six sessions with older people from the local community, one older person working with a group of four or five children at a time:

Session 1: A general introductory session on life in the 1920s and 1930s with the children being asked to discover when and where the pensioners were born, what their birthplace was like in their childhood, and details of family background. The pensioners were asked to construct their own family tree, a task for which the children had been prepared in class previously. The session was followed up after the pensioners' visit by a class discussion session on old age.

Session 2: This concentrated on home life when older people were young – housing, furnishing, housework, cooking, etc. – followed up by a comparison with conditions in the children's own homes today.

Session 3: This session was attended by a museum worker who brought a collection of slides and items to be handled and discussed by the children and older people together. Items related back to the previous week's session.

Session 4: This session concentrated on schooling in the 1920s and 1930s, and made use of photographs from the period. Each group of children explored different questions with a pensioner. For instance: What were teachers like? What were classrooms like? What did a typical school day consist of? What was the pensioner's favourite lesson? Was there uniform? School meals? Music, art and PE? What happened to 'naughty' children? The class finally had to decide whether they would have liked to go to school at that time.

Session 5: This session dealt with sports, games and entertainments and the differences between then and now. This offered the opportunity to introduce actual toys from the period and try out both toys and games: diabolo, whip and top, peevers (hopscotch), etc.

Session 6: This session dealt with dress and fashion, using period and modern photographs; discussing differences and similarities; the cost of clothing; how much was made at home using knitting and sewing patterns before the war, and how much time this took; and how common it was to have new clothes bought.

At the end of the project all the participants were asked to complete an evaluation sheet which asked four questions: Had they enjoyed the project? Could they write down what they enjoyed most? Did they think it was a good idea for young and old people to work together in this way? And, if so, could they explain why they thought so?

The school staff analysed the 'whole-curriculum' aspects of the project in the following way:

Language work: Stories and poems of the period, poetry of the First World War, an imaginary letter home from a soldier and a reply, reports on hobbies and pastimes of the 1920s, a speech on 'Votes for Women', and as a reading text 'The Bonnie Pit Laddie' by Frederick Grice.

Art/craft: War posters, model Edwardian village, fashion charts, 'In the trenches', and Edwardian house.

Religious education: The Temperance movement, changes in religion and Sunday observance.

PE/health education: Dances of the 1920s and 1930s, advances in medicine in the 1920s.

Maths: The 'old' money system, 1920s budgeting using a computer program.

Music: Songs of the period.

Geography: Town planning in the 1920s and 1930s, coal-mining areas and methods then and now.

History: Development of transport in the 1920s, education, some famous people from the period, the First World War, social conditions and fashion.

Science: The introduction of electric light, *Diary of an Edwardian Lady*, nature of the period.

Visits/broadcasts: 'How We Used to Live' TV programmes, pensioners' visits to school, visit to People's Palace, Glasgow, talk by visitor from Royal Scottish Museum with artefact.

The conclusion to the project took the form of a drama production which included a 'suffragette's' speech, a classroom scene, playground games, a fashion parade, and songs and dances from the period.

PRESTON STREET SCHOOL, EDINBURGH

The completion of a renovation programme inspired Preston Street School to celebrate its ninetieth birthday with a history project based on the school itself. The school log and Board minutes provided material on the school's earliest days, but older people from the local community were involved in a major reminiscence project to obtain first-hand information on what the school had been like in its early days with 800 pupils. It now houses 200!

Documents dating from the school's foundation were available (see Figure 15), and photographs from as early as 1915 were traced. An appeal in the local Press for information and exhibits made possible an exhibition on the school's history which attracted hundreds of local residents and former pupils. A reconstructed classroom, complete with slates and slate-pencils, was greatly appreciated and stimulated vivid memories (see Figure 16).

A reminiscence group was established at the local community

TRUANCY, 1890'S STYLE

Truancy is not just a problem of our own times, as these extracts from the school log show. Indeed, it seems as if a bit of seasonal absenteeism over Christmas and New Year was part of the routine.

November 8–12 1897 Separated three confirmed truants (Boyle, Fisher and Hogg) from their classes and kept them by themselves on Monday, Tuesday and Wednesday. No effect – on Thursday, all off, except Fisher who had been brought up by his mother and locked up by her in the Gymnasium, without any one being told. He was found there a little after 1 pm, when the room chanced to be opened. I wrote at once to the mother pointing out the danger of doing as she had done and warning her never to do so again. The boy on being allowed to the playground went off at once and has not since returned.

Dec 27–30 1897 Attendance thin on account of the holiday season. Many children going messages for bakers, grocers etc.

Dec 19–23 1898 Attendance fairly good. Work going on as usual. Called at the homes of a number of absentees and spoke to the parents.

Jan 3–6 1899 School reopened. 190 absent = 22%. On Friday 207 absent = 24%. Usual work done. Closed on Friday at 1.30pm, as a number of the pupils got 'Courant Fund' tickets for a New Year treat in the afternoon.

Jan 9–13 1899 Attendance not good, but gradually improved up to Thursday. Work going smoothly on. Wrote many parents about irregular children.

Figure 15   *Preston Street School, Edinburgh, celebrated its 90th anniversary with a history project based on the school's earliest days. The school logbook provided some interesting facts about truancy.*

LOOKING BACK AT...

SCHOOLDAYS AT PRESTON STREET

Rachel: You sat two to a desk and you had slots where your slate went in.

Ina: Your pride and joy was if you got a little Oxo can and you kept a damp sponge in it to clean your slate.

George: The slate pencils used to squeak. You got some with a bit of a false material in it, maybe a stone, and it went *!?*!@! You got a rap on the knuckles if you did that.

Nellie: Then my name was Nellie McKay. My initials was H.A.M. – Helen Anderson McKay. And I sat beside Edith Gordon Green. And her initials was E.G.G. – ham and egg!

We had a Mr Hunter. And there was a Mrs Stewart, she played the piano for us all marching into school. And there was a Miss Linton, she was the sewing teacher.

We only had a reading book and an arithmetic book. And a jotter. And a

> The voices of: Rachel Allardice, Nellie Benzie, George Carmichael, Alex Chalmers, Margaret Davies, Austin Deighton, Irene Innes, Nan Lumsden, Betty MacDougall, Ina Quinn, Jessie Ramage.

composition book. The teacher gave the pens oot. She kept them and she gave the pens oot and took them back again. And you got a new nib sometimes. If ye were awfy clever or the best you got to fill the inkwells and aw that kind o thing. If ye were the teachers pet.

Ina: The teachers were completely removed from you. You never thought they were humans that went home. You just thought that they disappeared into the cupboards when you weren't there.

Nellie: You had the same teacher when you went to the school at five, you had Miss Annie Mean or Miss Jessie Mean till you left the babies. It was the first babies, second babies, third babies, and then you went up the stairs into yon room just at the ladies – when you went in the girls door there was a room and that was Mrs Morrison, she was the next teacher. And you got her for a long time then when you went up the stair ye got either Mr Hunter or Mr Bell. Until ye left.

Figure 16 *Older people from the local community provided first-hand information on what Preston Street School had been like with vivid memories of their own schooldays.*

centre. 'Reliving parts of our childhood, we recalled the social patterns of sixty years ago, conditions were very different and as we discussed this many happy memories came flooding back – running neighbours' messages, minding babies, delivering morning milk, the Sunday School and the Band of Hope,' wrote Margaret Davies in the glossy booklet *Memories of Preston St. School and The Southside*, which was published to celebrate the anniversary.

The Community Education Service became involved in running a joint project that brought together at the Community Centre a primary Class 5 and its teacher from the school and former pupils. They met once a week to reminisce – mainly about the school and childhood but also about the history of the area.

> In an additional weekly session, about half-a-dozen members of this group met with the class. Objects were used to spark off older people's memories and the children's curiosity. For the session on childhood games we got everyone involved in trying out some of the old-style games we'd been talking about that week. The children thoroughly enjoyed it and discovered skills they did not know that they had in catching a diabolo or birling a top. Hopefully the basis has been laid for similar work in future involving children, teachers and old people.

LAMB'S HOUSE DAY CENTRE, LEITH

The Centre is run by Edinburgh District Council and has a tradition of working with local primary schools. Children from local schools visited the centre to 'play the games their grannie and granda played in the street'.

> From bools in the gutter, peeries and peevers on the paving stones, yo-yos in the hand and diabolos in the air, there was plenty of action. 'Cross-the-street' games were energetic and the boys tried to master duelling games while the girls were skipping and bouncing balls endlessly. All this happened with old people encouraging and acting as referees. It was great fun for all ages and everyone enjoyed themselves.
> (*Report in* Art Lines, *Edinburgh District Council*)

The following year, children were invited to play singing games, which they did with similar enthusiasm. As a result of these initiatives, a group was set up in Leith to collect all the games, songs, skipping and ball-game rhymes which used to be played in the local streets, with melodies and variations in words and rules, using the recollections of local older people.

GRANTON PRIMARY SCHOOL, LEITH

The school became involved in the Leith Local History Project with two local arts and theatre groups. The whole project was based on the memories and reminiscences of local residents in the port since the turn of the century. Pupils took photographs of modern Leith to compare to historical photographs provided by older people. They took part in drama activities, trying out 1920s clothes, games and school discipline.

> The children have learned a tremendous amount about how children in the 1920s could entertain themselves without very much equipment – and how they respected authority. I believe the project is probably the most important thing being done in linking young people with their grandparents and with older people. The children respond so well to the warm reaction of the old folk.
> (*Mrs Pat Donald, Project chairman*)

YORKSHIRE TELEVISION'S *THE WAY WE USED TO LIVE*

This is a very popular history series designed for 8- to 14-year-olds in school. Although now dealing with the early Victorian period, it previously concentrated on more recent history and has, according to the producer Ian Fell, had a significant impact beyond the conventional history syllabus in schools and with viewers considerably older than the age group at which it is aimed.

Mr Fell was pleased to learn from the senior occupational therapist for the York area health authority that the programme was being widely and successfully used in reminiscence therapy in local old people's homes and hospitals. Schools were also developing intergenerational projects as a direct result of the early series of *How We Used To Live*, and in 1985 the Midland Bank sponsored a competition for dramatic work arising out of the programme which attracted entrants from all over the country, some of which had involved work with older people in the schools' communities.

Chapter 5

Working with Local Authorities

Local education authorities, in spite of recent financial constraints, have not been unsympathetic to the principle of intergenerational projects. A LinkAge survey of links between schools, community education, and older people in Oxfordshire was commissioned by the local authority. The final report (*Harvest Gifts*, July 1991) was published by the authority and distributed to all schools and education centres. It included recommendations for further development.

Some local authorities, like Somerset and Lothian, have long-standing fully worked-out policies which emphasize that schools are resources for all age groups in the community. Others have preferred to channel their support through charities like LinkAge and Age Exchange.

There are many local education authorities which have shown some commitment to intergenerational work. However, the Lothian Regional Council in Scotland appears to have one of the longest and strongest records of experiment in the field.

Lothian came to prominence in the field of intergenerational work through a combination of circumstances and personalities which is probably unique. As long ago as 1978, the Regional Council decided to take advantage of falling rolls in its schools by encouraging the enrolment of adults for cultural studies, for basic education, and in school classes leading to examinations.

At the same time it began to open a series of purpose-built 'community high schools', where provision for adult users was specifically made on, or attached to, school premises. There are now seven officially designated community high schools in the region and a number of others, such as Beeslack High School in Penicuik, which have some accommodation for and/or commitment to adult education.

By 1987, when the commitment to the Open Door policy which encouraged adults into schools was confirmed by the education committee, thirty-one of the region's fifty-one high schools had enrolled adults. Some were doing this on an 'in-fill' basis, enrolling adults without charge into mainly examination classes when there were places available. Others had begun to offer separate classes, at a small fee, for examination courses and for a range of creative and recreational subjects.

In August 1987 all secondary schools were asked by the director of education to prepare a plan to receive adults into school. This plan was implemented, with old age pensioners and people in receipt of state benefits receiving concessions in the payment of fees.

Each Scottish Region has a Community Education Service which runs community centres staffed by trained community education workers providing opportunities and facilities for adults and young people and a wide range of other adult education provision. In 1982 a Community Education working party was set up in Lothian to develop educational opportunities for older people. It was felt that, at a time when the proportion of older people in the population was rising, opportunities should be provided for them to take part in educational activities if they wished. These included activities to promote creativity, survival skills, self-esteem and companionship, as well as more intellectual classes. The working party recognized intergenerational work specifically as a fruitful way of promoting education for older people in its widest sense – cognitive, creative, recreational, and social.

In December 1984 a national conference on intergenerational work was held in Edinburgh. David Sinclair, of the Lothian Community Education Service, pin-pointed one of the themes of the conference when he said that a community educator's response had to be based not only on the needs of older people but also on the contribution that they could make.

In 1986 Lothian established the Young and Old Together Steering Group, with adviser Roy Wilsher in the chair and Hilary Kirkland, co-ordinator for older people in the Community Education Service and a prime mover in the Edinburgh Conference two years earlier, as secretary. This group organized regional seminars, logged intergenerational work already being undertaken, organized exhibitions around what was already going on, and aimed to encourage new initiatives. An early success was the Celebrating Age Week in 1987, which encouraged a large number of the region's schools and community centres to take initiatives which brought old and young together, often for the first time in a particular community.

Some centres offered little more than a token gesture – inviting older people to harvest festival services, for instance – but others were more innovative. Cousland Primary School involved its children and local older people in the production of a 'Domesday disc' on village life. Lorne Primary School ran a session for young and old on 'Dancing Through Time'. Cuiken Primary School ran a Royal Mile discovery tour for young and old through Edinburgh's tourist centre.

Community education workers were not always directly involved in these initiatives, but in summing up the success of the week, David Sinclair concluded that his department's staff had given valuable support to schools and other groups as initiators, disseminators of information, resource providers, and evaluators.

The Young and Old Together Group was disbanded in 1989 partly because of financial restraints and partly because it was felt that it had achieved its objective of raising awareness of intergenerational work.

It left a legacy of an information pack and 'Resource Boxes' for 'Young and Old Together' which schools and community centres could borrow as and when they wished in order to take their work further or begin new projects.

In 1989 a working party of regional councillors set up to reassess the role, remit, and strategy of the Lothian Community Education Service reported (the Muir Report). It gave credit to the significant developments which had taken place in working with older people. Amongst its recommendations was a continuation of 'experimentation in family and intergenerational work as part of the overall youth provision'. The committee said that it would 'wish to see moves to create better understanding and joint project work where each member and each age group contributes toward achieving common objectives'. Although much of the work already done in Lothian had been initiated by those working with older people, the Muir Report firmly placed intergenerational work into the region's youth provision as well.

Lothian Community Education Service is currently working to encourage youth workers to make intergenerational work a priority, and to organize an international study tour for young and old together.

It is clear that much of the development work done in Lothian is now being used as a source and a model by other workers in the field both in the UK and abroad.

From its launch in 1988 by Lord Young of Dartington, the charity LinkAge has attempted to work as closely as possible with local authorities. The aim of LinkAge is to try to restore some of the advantages of the extended family to young and old in ways which are suited to the present day. In January 1990 the LinkAge project became part of CSV with the LinkAge Trust remaining responsible for funding and possible new work.

LinkAge has received funding from national charities and trusts (Gulbenkian, Paul Hamlyn, Telethon, Help the Aged, Age Concern, Baring Foundation, and the Institute of Community Studies) but has relied for community project backing on local sources and help from local authorities. As well as direct grants there has been a great deal of time and commitment from officials, teachers, and community education staff.

Co-operation between a local authority and LinkAge has been closest in the London Borough of Tower Hamlets, where the charity has been asked to investigate the possibility of developing a self-sustaining network for intergenerational work integrated within existing health, education, and social services. Gaps in service can often be filled in an imaginative way by using a Link-Age model. For example, the Social Services Occupational Therapy team work with elderly clients in their homes and in the process build a relationship with clients' carers. They may be aware of the bereavement and loneliness of a carer left behind but can do little to alleviate such problems. A referral to a pensioners' lunch club may not be enough for some who are used to an active life and wish to remain active. A referral system where they can be linked to a school may be more beneficial if they are attracted to helping and mixing with young people.

This project led to detailed discussions with education officials and a survey of schools to discover what intergenerational projects already existed and how schools could move into the field or extend existing work. Suggestions were received with enthusiasm and most selected a programme of activities which suited their individual needs.

Ecology has proved a popular basis for school projects linking young people and older volunteers in an inner-city area with few green spaces. Schools have also shown enthusiasm for the idea of inviting older members of the ethnic minority communities into schools. Many schools felt that their ethnic minority pupils lacked older role models and would benefit from storytelling in their mother tongues, reminiscence about life in their families' country of origin, and help in building cross-cultural links across the whole school.

LinkAge's function in Tower Hamlets has been as a link between schools and other institutions. It is hoped that Tower Hamlets will become a model for other local authorities.

Age Exchange is another charity which has received considerable funding from local authorities and which has worked in the fields of health and social services as well as in education. The Age Exchange Reminiscence Centre stands right in the centre of Blackheath Village in south-east London, and is the focus of constant comings and goings by older people and the young. Inside visitors enter a lost world: a complete wooden shop interior which is a wonderland of drawers and biscuit tins and jars where half-forgotten consumer items such as dolly blue and gob-stoppers rub shoulders with the sort of kitchen range on which our grandmothers cooked and baked, heated the iron and warmed the babies' bottles. The shop-floor is narrow and congested, crammed to the ceiling with memorabilia from a domestic past which has already almost completely faded from most people's memories. Behind the 'shop' is studio space which is used for theatrical performances, workshops, and exhibitions on a range of historical themes from Cycling Days (part of the Greenwich Festival), to Caribbean Recipes and Remedies, which was supported by the Commission for Racial Equality, and an exhibition on Jewish East End weddings.

Age Exchange's approach is both multi-media and multi-age. It grew essentially out of reminiscence work with older people, which has resulted in a range of books based upon the recollections of old people about their lives. Titles include *Fifty Years Ago*, *All Our Christmases*, *Can We Afford the Doctor?* and *On the River*. Reminiscences were also used as scripts for musical entertainments which have toured widely in old people's homes, in community centres, and in hospitals and schools both in London and further afield.

Age Exchange has been funded from a variety of sources, including several London boroughs, health and educational charities, industry and commerce, and trades unions. An increasing, though small, proportion of its income comes from sales of its own books and other fees it is able to generate from its training and educational activities. The interest of the Inner London Education Authority, and subsequently a grant from Telethon, enabled it to extend its work with older people into the intergenerational field. It runs a regular youth theatre and works with schoolchildren both at the Reminiscence Centre, which is regarded as a valuable history resource by local schools, and in classrooms. Future funding for education projects is being sought.

Age Exchange has built up a large and enthusiastic group of volunteers who play an active part in running the Reminiscence Centre. They organize social events and help with the many parties of young visitors who come from schools all over south and east London. The museum at the Centre is not a conventional one. Children can touch the exhibits and try them out, discovering just how different and sometimes difficult life was in the period before widespread domestic 'automation'. Volunteers are on hand to show children how things worked and just what it was like using them.

The Centre also has Reminiscence Boxes, which can be borrowed by schools or groups for older people. A box will include both written material and objects which can stimulate reminiscence and further discussion: for instance, a collection of items used for cooking, or on wash-day, or a selection of remedies and potions from a 1930s or 1940s chemist's shop. Smell and touch are not forgotten in providing for older people whose eyesight may no longer be very good. Who can ever forget the smell of camphorated oil?

Age Exchange is clearly untypical in that it has so far succeeded in obtaining funding which has enabled it to employ professional staff and to work on a scale which cuts across local authority boundaries and is occasionally national in its impact. It brings together reminiscence, theatre in education, publishing, and a museum and an exhibition centre in a unique combination which would be difficult to emulate elsewhere. It is involved not only in intergenerational work but also in reminiscence work in old people's homes and geriatric hospitals, and runs an extensive training programme for care staff. Even so, much of its experience must be of interest to schools, though they may have to work on a much smaller scale.

Charities like LinkAge and Age Exchange have proved that there is an immense fund of goodwill towards the idea of bringing young and old together in creative projects which benefit both generations. They have been able to attract support from local education authorities in the form of direct grants and organizational support and assistance. It is extremely worrying that in the present crisis in local authority finance, support for all sorts of community education, including intergenerational projects, may be put in jeopardy.

In Scotland too, where the existence of Regional Community Education Services – responsible for adult education, youth work and community development – has proved to be immensely beneficial to the development of intergenerational work, financial constraints in some regions threaten the continuation of community education. Lothian's policy and practice have developed largely as a result of community education initiatives, and every effort is being made to maintain and build on what is now a substantial and well-proven methodology, despite hard times.

Chapter 6

Conclusions

Intergenerational projects are one of those ideas that occasionally come up from the grass-roots of education without very much encouragement or support from the centre. They flourish now in the United States, and similar projects are being explored in several European countries.

In Britain, too, there has been an explosion of interest during the 1980s and early 1990s. Without exception, those involved in them praise them highly for their beneficial effects – on both the children and young people and the older people who have been involved. Why is this? Although there has been no major research done on intergenerational work in this country (the United States is investing millions of dollars in this field) there are some conclusions being drawn by some of those involved which are also inherent in the case studies.

The first conclusion to be drawn from the case studies in this book is that intergenerational projects of all sorts have been pursued with enormous enthusiasm by participants of all ages. Some, like the Heritage project at Arran High School, have now continued for a decade or more and have brought wide-ranging benefits. As Maureen Farquharson at Arran sums it up, the project there has linked the school more firmly than anyone anticipated to its local community, and has given the older generation on the island both a sense that their history is valued and the opportunity to participate in the education of the island's children.

Other projects, like the initiative at Dunstan Riverside Primary School in Gateshead, have grown from rather tentative beginnings to the point where up to eighty older people may be in school during a week and a majority of the school's pupils have become involved in one way or another. The description of how one project led to another is typical of the knock-on effect apparent in many of the schools once the initial contact between the generations has been made.

The case studies also offer many projects in which encouraging children and young people to move out of school to make contact with older people in the community has led to long-term and warmly appreciated involvement. The close relationship between St John's Primary School and the residents of Bethnal Green Hospital is just one example of the possibilities which open up when teachers and care workers realize the potential benefits of bringing the generations together, even where the older people involved are relatively frail.

Obviously this is an area into which educational professionals need to move gently and with some sensitivity. Both young people and older people harbour many misconceptions about each other in a society which is increasingly segregated by age. Stereotypes exist that may take time and patience to break down.

Not least amongst the stereotypes are the racial ones which plague our society. But even these are not insuperable. Amongst the projects described here, there are several where highly successful relationships have been built up between children from ethnic minority communities and older people whose families have lived for several, if not many, generations in areas like East London. Initial worries on the part of the children's teachers that they might meet prejudice happily proved unfounded. But race is a factor which obviously will have to be carefully considered when trying to bridge the generation gap.

Equally the existence of different minority groups in an area must lead some schools to consider how far they should try to make contact with the older people of the minority communities themselves, particularly if the school serves their grandchildren. It is not necessarily the case, as the stereotype has it, that minority communities find it easy to 'look after their old people so much better'. The confused, the sick, the lonely, and 'young' old people with something to offer are, no doubt, with us all, and ethnic minority communities in Britain may welcome involvement in intergenerational projects.

It is significant that LinkAge's contacts in Tower Hamlets have revealed a real desire amongst the ethnic minority communities themselves for increased involvement in intergenerational work in the schools and elsewhere. Older members of these communities are sometimes amongst the most isolated, with language difficulties compounding the common problems of old age.

Teachers should also be aware that there may be some nervousness amongst the older generation about venturing into schools at all, partly because their own experiences at school may have been mainly negative ones and partly because they believe, rightly, that schools have changed very significantly since they themselves left them. There can be a deep ambivalence amongst older people who were themselves disciplined with the cane or the tawse at the sight of youngsters who are rather happier for not having that threat hanging over them. But as Peter Davies, former head of Icknield School in Oxfordshire, points out, once older people are in a school their natural interest in what is going on is soon aroused and leads them quite naturally into closer involvement.

Of course, in some circumstances relationships between young and old are difficult to make. Older people who are confused, who have physical and mental handicaps, who may not even be able to speak clearly or coherently, are a challenge for children who may have had no regular contact with older people before they visit an old people's home or geriatric ward. But many of the experiences recounted in this book show that children can triumph over the disabilities of older people. This may not always be done without a little initial distress or embarrassment, as the experience recorded as part of the Behind Wise Eyes project in Dorset illustrates. But initial communication difficulties were overcome, and by the end of the project both sides – young and old – were appreciative of the contacts and relationships which had been made.

One conclusion which runs through most of the evaluation of intergenerational work is that time spent on preparation with old and young separately is never likely to be time wasted. It may be essential to the success of the project. Even further, it may only be through the setting of clear objectives and some assessment of attitudes before and after a project that it is possible to judge whether anything has been gained from it at all.

Equally, evaluation itself is important. It was surprising to find how many busy teachers involved in intergenerational projects featured in this book had found the time to assess the elements of success and failure in what they had been doing. By its very nature, an intergenerational project risks having one generation 'use' the other. Constant vigilance is needed to ensure that no one is being exploited or patronized or even, and there is that very slight risk, abused.

Feedback for the participants is important too. Older people who have been involved in work with a school deserve at the very least to be invited to see any exhibition of work or performance which resulted and to receive copies of any publications. As many of the case studies show, older people take enormous pleasure from seeing their experiences recorded by children in written work and pictures, drama and song, and in seeing the finished products of any other school work in which they may have been involved as helpers or participants. At its Reminiscence Centre, Age Exchange always displays children's work which has arisen out of intergenerational contacts so that older people who have worked on a project can see how their ideas and experiences have been developed by the younger generation.

Those involved in reminiscence work constantly emphasize the real pride older people take in their own histories, especially when they see them reproduced and evidently valued by another generation. What is most clear from the work of an organization like Age Exchange is the pleasure its beautifully produced publications give to those who have contributed to them.

There are other lessons to be drawn from intergenerational work. Most of those who have had experience of successful projects emphasize three points:

1. Good practice should break down and not reinforce the stereotypes both generations may hold of the other.
2. Projects should involve both generations mutually so that

neither is seen in an exclusively 'giving' or 'helping' role –
as may sometimes happen if, for instance, teenagers simply
descend on old people to undertake decorating or gardening,
or if older volunteers come into school to 'help' without
investing time in building up relationships with the children
they are there for.

3. Projects should consciously promote a positive approach to
old age and consciously help young people to come to terms
with the ageing process and recognize the benefits which age
and experience can bring.

There are, concludes Margaret Macdonald, who has made a
study of intergenerational work in Scotland, positive psychological benefits to both generations in such projects. Older people
gain from a renewed sense that they are needed, that they can
learn new skills and gain new interests, and that they can pass on
some of the lessons of experience to a new generation while at the
same time learning from them.

The young gain from having their evident fear of old age
broken down by close contact with older people, while at the
same time being stimulated by the range and richness of older
people's experience, and challenged to consider the value of
learning itself in the light of older people's high regard for the
process.

Other benefits are academic. No less a historian than Raymond
Williams makes the point strongly in *The Long Revolution* that
it is important for the history of ordinary people to be recorded.
'Living witnesses', he argues, are the key to recording how life
really was in each generation for people who conventionally have
never found a place in formal history books. Tape, video and
film can now be used quite cheaply to augment the printed word
and schoolchildren can relatively easily acquire the skills to help
make a living record of, to use Yorkshire Television's phrase,
'how we used to live'. The archives have already been greatly
enriched by some of the intergenerational work based on reminiscence which has happened in various parts of the country.

Intergenerational work does, of course, raise questions of
funding. There are projects which have been launched entirely
at the initiative of an individual school or facility for older

people. But most of the projects described here have involved a 'third party': a co-ordinator from an organization such as LinkAge or Help the Aged, a community education worker based either in school or neighbouring community centre, or the quite extensive resources of an organization such as Age Exchange. Others have been launched with the help of a teacher given the opportunity to do so through some form of 'community' allocation of time during the normal school week. Funding, therefore, has been to a greater or lesser extent more generous than a school or other institution could normally find on its own.

Is this additional input essential? Obviously not – there are many examples in this book of projects which have been started and sustained through the efforts of an individual teacher or school. Which is not to say that third-party liaison cannot be extremely useful, especially in a climate where there are so many other pressures on teachers and workers with older people and where it may be increasingly difficult to find the time to launch and promote intergenerational schemes without help.

The answer to this problem may, however, lie in intergenerational co-operation itself. It is a mistake to regard intergenerational work as only involving the very aged and possibly frail. Volunteer organizations such as RSVP, as we have seen, are very successfully harnessing the time and energy of retired people who may, for various reasons, be as young as 50. These are people who can, as Age Exchange has found at its Reminiscence Centre in Blackheath, provide some of the person-power to organize and run many aspects of intergenerational work themselves. In this way, the burden can be lifted from the professionals, and talent and organizational skills be incidentally harnessed – to the immense satisfaction of those who, although technically retired, still feel that they have much to offer the community.

Concern with logistics and funding will necessarily be at the forefront of the minds of any teachers reading this book and wondering whether or not they can follow the example of so many of their colleagues up and down the country by trying to bring their children into contact with the older generation in their community. But all the evidence is that if schools are convinced of the enormous benefits which can accrue to older and younger people from intergenerational projects – as they surely must be if they have read this book – they can overcome difficulties and get projects off the ground in the most unlikely circumstances.

And it would be wrong not to end with some of the people, very old and very young, who have already been involved in projects. In Edinburgh, there was Mrs Pratt whose young friends call her Chrissie and pop in to see her on their way home from school. On a chilly station platform in East London there was a former teacher who found that with young children he regained the confidence to try to talk again after a stroke. And there was Mary, who died in Bethnal Green Hospital, visited to the last by schoolchildren who now cherish her Pink Panther in their classroom. The relationships are those which children ought to have with their own grandparents but which many, separated by geography or family breakdown, do not have. For many workers in the field, the relationships are what make it, more than anything, immensely worth while.

Appendix

Sources of Further Help and Information

Age Concern England
1268 London Road,
London SW16 4ER. Tel: 081–679 8000
Age Exchange
The Reminiscence Centre,
11 Blackheath Village,
London SE3 9LA. Tel: 081–318 9105
Age Resource
1268 London Road,
London SW16 4ER. Tel: 081–679 2201
All Change Arts (Community drama/arts)
177 Upper Street,
Islington,
London N1 1RG. Tel: 071–359 9585
Centre for Policy on Ageing
25–31 Ironmonger Row,
London EC1V 3QP. Tel: 071–253 1787
Community Education Development Centre
Lyna Hall,
Blackberry Lane,
Coventry CV2 3JS. Tel: 0203 638660
Community Service Volunteers Education
237 Pentonville Road,
London N1 9NJ. Tel: 071–278 6601
Help the Aged
St James's Walk,
London EC1R 0BE. Tel: 071–253 0253

LinkAge CSV
237 Pentonville Road,
London N1 9NJ. Tel: 071–278 6601
Magic Me
Mile End Hospital,
Bancroft Road,
London E1 4DG. Tel: 071–377 7878
Pensioners' Link
405–407 Holloway Road
London N7 6HJ. Tel: 071–700 4070
Retired and Senior Volunteer Programme (RSVP)
237 Pentonville Road,
London N1 9NJ. Tel: 071–278 6601
Scottish Community Education Council
West Coates House,
90 Haymarket Terrace,
Edinburgh EH12 5LQ. Tel: 031–313 2488

BOOKS, PAMPHLETS, VIDEOS, ETC.

Available from CSV Education:

1. A revised version of *Life After 60: Growing Old in Britain Today*. Work-cards and exercises aimed at breaking down stereotypes (CSV and Age Concern, 1988).
2. *Open Doors: Elderly People as Volunteers in Primary Schools* (CSV, 1987).
3. *Opening Doors: Community Projects in Primary Schools* (CSV, 1984).

Others:

Harvest Gifts: a report by LinkAge on links between schools, community education and older people in Oxfordshire, available from Oxfordshire County Council Education Service, Macclesfield House, Oxford, or LinkAge.

Behind Wise Eyes booklet and video are available from South West Arts, Bradninch Place, Gandy Street, Exeter EX4 3LS, as a set for £12, or separately for £4 and £11.50.

Somerset County Council has produced a video on its community school initiatives, 'The School Belongs to All of Us', which is available from Somerset County Council, Community Education Training and Development, Park Road, Bridgwater, Somerset TA6 7HS.

Older Learners: the challenge to adult education, Susanna Johnston and

Chris Phillipson (eds), Bedford Square Press/NCVO, 1983.
Parents, Schools and Community: working together in health information, HEC Slow Learners Project, 1987.
Memories and Things: linking museums and libraries with older people, WEA (SE Scotland District) 1988; £3.50 from WEA, Riddles Court, 322 Lawnmarket, Edinburgh.
Children Growing Up: a guide to teaching elderly people about child development, International Federation on Ageing, 1987.
Who Cares about Elderly People? Child's Play (Int. Ltd.), 1989.
Recall: a tape/slide programme in three parts designed to stimulate and aid reminiscence. Available from Help the Aged, price £23.50.
Ageing today . . . and tomorrow, Age Concern.

Age Exchange Publications:

A Place to Stay: multicultural reminiscences of schooldays in the 1920s and 1930s.
Good-night Children Everywhere: memories of evacuation in the Second World War.
When We Were Young: rural reminiscences, including intergenerational work, from a Somerset reminiscence project.
Other titles also available.
Available for hire: portable exhibitions of photos and memories on different themes, and Reminiscence Boxes for use with mixed groups of older and younger people.

LinkAge

Training and information pack, designed to help those working with either the young or old start an intergenerational project with confidence and inspiration.

Index